D1525778

The
Insanity
of
Normality

ALSO BY ARNO GRUEN

The Betrayal of the Self:
The Fear of Autonomy in Men and Women

The Insanity of Normality

REALISM AS SICKNESS:
TOWARD UNDERSTANDING
HUMAN DESTRUCTIVENESS

ARNO GRUEN

Translated from the German by
Hildegarde and Hunter Hannum

GROVE WEIDENFELD
New York

Published by Grove Weidenfeld
A division of Grove Press, Inc.
841 Broadway
New York, NY 10003-4793

Published in Canada by General Publishing Company, Ltd.

Originally published in Germany by Kösel Verlag under the
title *Der Wahnsinn der Normalität—Realismus als Krankheit:
eine grundlegende Theorie zur menschlichen Destruktivität.*

Occasional deviations from the German original
are at the author's request.

Excerpts from Henrik Ibsen's *Peer Gynt*, translated by
Michael Meyer, are reprinted by permission of Harold Ober
Associates Incorporated. Copyright © 1963, 1991 by Michael Meyer

Library of Congress Cataloging-in-Publication Data

Gruen, Arno.
[Wahnsinn der Normalität. English]
The insanity of normality : realism as sickness: toward understanding
human destructiveness /
Arno Gruen ; translated from the German by Hildegarde and Hunter
Hannum.—1st English language ed.
p.   cm.
Translation of: Wahnsinn der Normalität.
Includes bibliographical references and index.
ISBN 0-8021-1169-6 (alk. paper)
1. Violence—Etiology. 2. Autonomy (Psychology) 3. Self.
4. Mental illness. I. Title.
RC569.5.V55G7813   1992
616.85'82071—dc20   91-38341
                                                          CIP

Manufactured in the United States of America
Designed by Irving Perkins Associates, Inc.
Printed on acid-free paper
First English-language Edition 1992
1   3   5   7   9   10   8   6   4   2

Contents

Preface

In the face of the calamities of the twentieth century, the issue of whether humankind is naturally good has never seemed more debatable. Sigmund Freud saw human beings as born with an ineradicable death wish, an innate predisposition toward violent and destructive behavior. This book was written in the hope that my experiences and observations could help people counter this rationalization of evil with their own truths. This work, therefore, is my reaction to what I will call "the insanity of realism," which in the name of love produces death and destruction.

It is an act of self-betrayal when children begin to lose consciousness of their own self. This process begins when they no longer perceive the feelings of their fathers and mothers directly but are guided by the way their parents see themselves. Such "adaptation" to the power needs of parents leads to a split in children's psychic structure, separating their interior world from its interactions with the environment. In this way, the connection and interplay between actions and motivations disappear. In order to be able to share in the power that subjugates them, children substitute obedience and adaptation for responsibility for their own actions. If we lose the connection to our own interior world, then we can relate only to a false self, to an image-oriented self attuned to behavior and feelings pleasing to our surrounding world. The need and perhaps also the compulsion to preserve this image-orientation take precedence over all one's own potential perceptions and feelings and empathy. The resulting inability to be rooted in oneself is what engenders destructive and evil behavior. That is the subject matter of this book.

I am, of course, not the first writer to deal with the subject of human destructiveness. As the Finnish psychoanalyst Martti Siirala, for example, puts it, among all living creatures human beings seem to be the only ones who destroy for destruction's sake—*as an end in itself.*[1] Whereas Sigmund Freud and Erich Fromm locate human destructiveness either in an a priori death instinct or in necrophilic tendencies stemming from stunted development at the anal or oedipal stage,[2] I believe I have found many indications that destructive and murderous behavior is rooted in the betrayal human beings commit against themselves in order to share in a hallucinated sense of power. Since there is no "higher fate" involved here but rather individuals who have cooperated more or less consciously in their own submission, a lifelong self-hatred ensues. The sad result is that only destructiveness imparts the feeling of aliveness.

In the first chapter I treat the question of responsibility and contrast it with what generally serves as its measure: the notions of duty and obedience. Proceeding from there, I arrive at a characterization of insanity that deviates from the one advanced by official psychology and psychiatry. The approach taken by these disciplines limits itself to judging human behavior exclusively according to the degree of a person's relatedness to reality. Naturally, such a view has validity; however, it prevents us from detecting a more subtle and dangerous form of pathology, one of whose symptoms is concealment: I refer to the type of insanity that disguises itself by hiding behind the mask of mental health. This insanity can easily conceal itself in a world in which deception and trickery are approved methods of adapting to reality.

Whereas people who can no longer bear the absence of human values in the real world are considered "crazy," those who have severed themselves from their human roots are certified "normal." And it is members of the latter group to whom we entrust power and whom we allow to determine our lives and our future. We believe they have the correct key to reality and know how best to deal with it. But a person's "relatedness to reality" is not the only criterion for establishing mental illness or health; we also have to ask to what degree feelings such as despair, perceptions such as empathy, and experiences such as enthusiasm are still possible.

The second chapter treats self-hatred and its origin: the Basic Lie that shrouds in silence the complicity in one's own submission. If we reject our self because it might endanger our position of power, vengeful feelings begin to determine our life. We insist upon being loved for causing others pain, an action frequently even interpreted as kindliness. (Early on, weren't we supposed to love our parents for inflicting pain upon us? Didn't they have our own good at heart?) A dissociated self cannot come to terms with its own submission and collaboration—therefore, parents' claims that their demands have sprung from love must be accepted and defended. It is in the name of this kind of parental "love" and "solicitude" that power over other people is established.

In this connection I adduce examples from the Third Reich because German fascism throws an especially clear light on phenomena existing wherever people are split off from their interior world. The end of the Third Reich by no means did away with the preconditions for such occurrences; the way a person *appears* is still prized above inner substance, and adaptation is still rewarded above inner independence. Today more than ever, these preconditions assume the appearance of humanitarianism and benevolence. Horrible intentions and acts are concealed more and more frequently behind smiling faces and masquerade as friendliness and seemingly considerate behavior. This is why it is especially difficult to recognize the actual pathology of our times.

In the third chapter I turn to the obsession with death. This obsession almost necessarily characterizes individuals who have suppressed their empathic ability. I proceed from the assumption that human development can take two basically different directions, one resulting in an inner life that maintains firm connections with the external world and one leading to an outer-directedness accompanied by surrender of one's interior world. If such an outer-directed development recognizes only obedience and adaptation and no longer acknowledges pain, the "natural" end product is destructive behavior. The bifurcation between inner- and outer-directed courses of development explains not only the two divergent paths of organization of the self; it also leads to two mutually exclusive realities: that of power and that of love.

Feelings that actually are not feelings are the subject of the fourth chapter, which addresses the problems associated with identification, a process that more often than we realize does not lead to an identity of one's own but to its avoidance.

I develop this question further in the fifth chapter, specifically with a view toward understanding the character of rebellion and conformity and their relationship to violence. I propose the thesis that many correspondences exist between the development of conformity and of rebellion and that these can be traced back to the individual's relationship to the "bad" mother. Whereas conformists defend the bad mother as the "good" mother, rebels seek out the good mother, although their actions stem from the influence of the bad mother.

How this influences the way the powerful exercise their power is shown in the sixth chapter. There I examine the American presidents Kennedy, Nixon, and Reagan and their foreign policies in this context.

In the seventh chapter I attempt to give a more accurate description of the psychopath, a type who represents for me the extreme opposite of the schizophrenic and who illustrates to the highest degree the insanity of apparent normality. Many readers will perhaps find it surprising yet extremely revealing to find this type personified by Henrik Ibsen's Peer Gynt, a figure from literature.

Finally, in the eighth chapter, I distinguish between the two opposite forms of insanity, insanity as a way of life and insanity as a protest against forms of social life and interpersonal relations felt to be unbearable. In our civilization the former is considered to be "realism" and only the latter an illness.

Some of the questions dealt with here have previously been touched upon in my book *The Betrayal of the Self.*[3] I return to them here not simply to repeat them but to explore them in greater depth.

It may strike the reader that I quite often refer to literature. In my opinion, literary works are closer to human reality than is, for instance, psychological research, which is much too strongly oriented toward the myth of realism and the power structures resulting from it. The artist, however, has not lost a connection to human needs and motives. Not the least of writers' reasons for writing is their desire to pit their creative powers against the deceptions of "prevailing opinion." They speak in a language that takes the totality of human experience into consideration.

On the other hand, the sciences, as Michael Polanyi has aptly described, attempt "to eliminate our human perspective from our picture of the world."[4] For this reason, the witness of writers to the totality as well as to the schizoid nature of human experience is of great importance to me. Their work often affords concrete examples of that insanity which, concealed behind the mask of health, is increasingly on the verge of delivering humankind over to self-destruction.

In order to illustrate my views with empirical cases, I sometimes turn to examples that may seem to represent extremes of human behavior. Perhaps some people will not find these examples significant, because their internal structure will not allow them to see the continuum running through the great diversity of human behavior. Such an attitude, however, simply mirrors the widespread denial of the ties that link us all together. It is essentially a logical maneuver intended to divert us from the continuum. The logic behind such splitting of human nature into categories and compartments merely serves to strengthen doubts about our totality and to make us insecure. The foundation of our wholeness lies in what our feelings and our heart tell us.

The language of the heart proceeds from our deep-seated needs for love and warmth, which we would like to give as well as receive. Our civilization, however, has made us anxious and ashamed if we feel vulnerable. The language of "reality" promises us relief from the "burden" of our needs, making us ready to stop trusting our own perceptions. This is why the language of the heart is our only salvation. Our fragmentation must be overcome not by acquiescing in the logic of an alleged "reality" but by insisting on our own ability to feel compassion, to experience sorrow and joy. That is one of the reasons I have written this book.

I would like to thank four friends for what they have contributed to this work, for the stimulation of their ideas as well as for the enrichment that knowing them has brought me. Two are extraordinary psychiatrists and psychoanalysts: Walter H. Lechler and Martti Siirala. The third, Aarne Siirala, is a theologian and philosopher. The deep empathic sensitivity of the fourth, Hans Krieger, has helped me a great deal in developing my ideas. Conversations with him also have helped me to clarify and express more precisely some of my trains of thought. I owe very much to the totality of thought and life of these friends. The same is true for Gaetano Benedetti, whose profound humaneness has opened up the way for our understanding of the schizophrenic and whose generosity has been a great support to me. Likewise, I owe a debt of gratitude to Ulrike Buergel-Goodwin, the editor of the original German edition of this work, whose enthusiasm and understanding were a great help to me in communicating my concerns.

They could beat a person to death, and they were absolutely normal while they were doing it—that I can't understand.
A former Polish concentration camp inmate

Good and evil are not determined by the intercourse of people with one another, but entirely by a man's relations with himself.
Jakob Wassermann

The
Insanity
of
Normality

I

The Denial of Reality in the Name of Realism

To BECOME RESPONSIBLE for one's own self is a paradoxical process. Those who think in terms of simple chronological time sequences will never grasp the mechanisms at work here. Development is inconceivable without external influences. We all have parents, who exert a determining influence on us throughout our lives. Yet the contradictions that arise within our inner psychic sphere develop a dynamism of their own. Thus, actions occur that are apparently determined by specific external events but in fact have little or nothing to do with them.

While environment influences the growing young self, a child's reactions to these formative influences, in turn, have an effect on the environment. What is involved here, then, is constant reciprocity. Father and mother can force their wills upon the child, but the type and intensity of their influence are also determined by their child's reactions.

The complexity of this interplay is apparent when we consider, on the one hand, that the possibility of autonomy is established in the earliest interactions between the growing self and its environment but, on the other hand, that the degree to which children take responsibility for themselves is a decisive factor in the process. All of a child's future relations within the surrounding social field depend on this. Basically, responsibility can develop in two directions: the evolving psyche either directs—openly and freely, answerable only to itself—the formation of its own self or it passively submits to the formative influences of others. In the latter case, it evades the burdens of true responsibility.

Escape from responsibility is always repressed from consciousness. Necessarily so, since the surrender of autonomy by submission to the will of another initiates a fundamental power game: "I will become the way you want me to be so that you'll take care of me. My submissiveness ensures my power over you from now on; with it I force you to take care of me." In this way, dependence becomes revenge for submissiveness. This act has several aspects. First, children accept their parents' evaluation of them without reservation; introjection is therefore a process of collaboration through submission.[1] Second, this means that children begin to hate everything in themselves that could bring them into conflict with parental expectations. And third, out of this self-hatred grows a readiness for ever more submission. Thus, a vicious circle is set in motion, with submission and self-contempt each giving rise to the other. In this situation, two things are always present: self-hatred and self-contempt. Yet they must not be felt, as that would be unbearable. For this reason, the whole process must remain unconscious; it is repressed and denied with the result that those involved fall blindly deeper and deeper into the snares of a power game.

The eternal reproach of someone who has yielded to the will of another is "You haven't done enough for me." This is an expression of the fantasized counterpower inherent in every pact based on dominance and submission. The power game is played in secret and begins in the preverbal flux of the infant's emotive life. It *must* remain hidden to conceal the fact that an intent to exercise counterpower is present. The hallucination of such a counterpower conceals from those who have surrendered themselves to others the fact that they have done so willingly. This leads to a double failure: their submissiveness remains intact and their revenge becomes self-destructive. The need for revenge, perpetually fueled by self-hatred for one's submission to the power and will of the parents, becomes the unacknowledged and unrecognized source and guiding motive of the individual's emotive life.

This is the way the human situation looks if collaboration in our own surrender characterizes our development. And those who no longer know that they have surrendered will not be able to reintegrate their dissociated self in later life. The resulting self-hatred will feed into all their subsequent actions in an attempt to compensate for their psychic imbalance. Only if we confront the self that has submitted so readily can we reduce—albeit painfully—our self-hatred. But to confront this self would mean acknowledging the submission that is the source of our hatred.

Children cannot recognize and thus cannot admit they have been unable to bear the pain of not having the self truly accepted and acknowledged. To feel oneself accepted by another's love is a basic prerequisite for human growth. The German dramatist Friedrich Hebbel expressed this in a poem:

> *Thus wondrously within your eyes*
> *I saw myself unfold.*

The pain of not being accepted is very likely involved in the so-called failure to thrive syndrome and in extreme cases can even lead to the death of infants.[2] Usually children submit in order to partake of the power oppressing them. Apparently, autistic children deal differently with this pain; they seem not to be prepared to deny it.[3]

It is paradoxical that we cannot live with self-hatred without doing something about it. To face it directly we would have to confront the pain of our self-betrayal. Therefore, we deny our self-hatred. The contradiction between the need to save face before ourselves and our willingness to ally ourselves with power by submission is therefore the most fundamental and perhaps the first dissociation in the human psyche. This is not just a case of repression but of a radical splitting off of awareness of our self-surrender and the resulting self-hatred, which then becomes a basic principle of our whole life. Such dissociation is maintained and abetted by a cultural ideology that equates obedience with responsibility: to be obedient is to be good and to be good is to be responsible. To be free, on the other hand, means being disobedient, and whoever is disobedient courts disapproval and jeopardizes the protection of the powerful and the chance of sharing their power.

At this point it is necessary to say something about the sociological view of human existence. Criminality, for example, is often seen as a result of poverty, yet this fails to explain why the majority of the poor do not become criminals. We must not deduce from this, however, that poverty is unrelated to criminality. One must discriminate here: if a hungry man steals, he is not acting out of greed, and if he involuntarily kills someone in the act, it is not premeditated murder. On the other hand, the rich and powerful belong to the group in our society that initiates wars, destroys livelihoods, and poisons nature and other human beings; nevertheless, these are not the people who populate our prisons. Official statistics on criminality include more poor people than rich because these statistics reflect the ideology of the rich and powerful and do not include all forms of destructiveness.

Our civilization with its demand for obedience is at the root of self-hatred; here lies the source of our malaise and unhappiness. Whenever we avoid facing truth for the sake of those ideologies that sustain our power-based culture, unhappiness will be a constant feature in our lives, no matter what the economic or political character of a given society may be.

The clearest sign of this is the revengeful and reproachful manner in which many people behave, regardless of whether they live in a capitalist or communist country. For revenge and reproach—not freedom—have become their goals in life; consequently, they increasingly intensify their dependency and fall prey to the illusion that power is the panacea for all problems. This is why so many people consistently hold fast to the lie that they can stand on their own two feet and are autonomous. This is also why every power play is hypocritical about its motives and is based on a lie about one's self. Thus, a mother ignoring her crying child (after all, she has just changed its diapers) will, rather than acknowledging her baby's despair, deny its need for closeness and pity herself instead. What is hidden here is her exercise of power over a helpless being.

Psychological changes cannot come about simply through an understanding of one's own history. In all types of psychotherapy or psychoanalysis the mere unraveling of the complex chronology of childhood experiences and influences does not suffice to produce genuine change. Patients change only when they accept responsibility for the decision they once made to submit to the power of others. For it is this submission that has crippled their potential for autonomy and initiated their psychic maldevelopment.

This is also the basis for my criticism of Alice Miller, although I consider her work important and significant (for example, *The Drama of the Gifted Child* and *For Your Own Good*). She contends that understanding one's developmental determinants is sufficient to bring about healing. In actual fact, this leads only to patients basking voluptuously in the mirror of the therapist's understanding without having to change themselves. And therapists, by feeling themselves to be the "good mother," do not have to recognize that they have made their patients dependent on them. In this way the eternal game is repeated between the powerful and their dependents, between the "good" mother and her grateful child, who consequently need not grow up. This internalization of the therapist—which is the opposite of finding one's own identity—is mistakenly considered being grown up.

Another form of crippling occurs when a person only feigns submission to others in order to defend her or his autonomy. This, however, is a paradoxical way of preserving at least the *potential* for autonomy.

The only way to find true liberation and the courage to meet the challenge of change is by confronting the pain caused by self-betrayal. It is not, as already stated, enough to understand one's own history, but it is just as insufficient merely to "understand" the social forces that influence the individual's development. That alone cannot explain why a person becomes a murderer. We must confront the surrender that first made us hate ourselves and then all life around us because it reminds us of what we have done. Evil, destructiveness, inhumanity—all have their roots in our inability to take responsibility for the early decision that made us relinquish our birthright to be ourselves. Of course, evil and inhumanity are impossible without those social structures and arrangements that mask our submission and dependency and equate obedience with "responsible" behavior. But as long as we see Hitler, for example, as a phenomenon that can be summed up by discursive categories such as "normal" or "mentally ill," we shall not be able to grasp what it meant and still means for us today that a man like him could come to power.

In light of the above, it should now be evident why I find it necessary to give a broader meaning to the concept of "mental illness." That is the only way to reach a comprehensive understanding of human beings and the psychological aberrations of which we are capable. What psychiatry and psychology classify as insanity is bound up with the notion of an increasing loss of connection to reality. A greater or lesser degree of relatedness to reality—all human behavior is measured by this yardstick. In this view, "reality" is understood exclusively as external reality.

Naturally, relatedness to reality—the degree of a person's allegiance to external reality—is a spectrum that makes it possible for us to classify human behavior along a line ranging from psychosis to neurosis to normality. Yet this scheme conceals the fact that another kind of insanity also exists that is much more dangerous than the one characterized by the loss of relatedness to reality.

To *see* this other kind of insanity we need to change our angle of vision and abandon the traditional categories. Then we can recognize that behind the orientation to "reality," which is the usual criterion of sanity, is concealed a more serious and less obvious form of pathology: that of "normal" behavior—the pathology of "adjustment" resulting from the surrender of the self.

If we examine this form of pathology more closely, the first thing to strike us is that it is an illness whose intention is not to produce insanity but to "trick" it: "to become so utterly sane that one does not know one is insane."[4] What I mean by the "intention" of an illness becomes clear, for example, in those conspicuous types of deviant behavior by means of which people try to call attention to their suffering. These are cries for help and are often so veiled that they only make those calling for help, as well as those to whom the cries are directed, more helpless than ever.[5] In contrast, what distinguishes the pathology of normality that tries to trick insanity is a flight from suffering. What we see here in exaggerated form is not only the flight from emotional pain but also the fear of falling apart that constantly threatens the cohesion of this type of personality.

It is not easy to illustrate this process, for our study of it is blocked by our ways of perceiving things. Hence, we are often impervious to certain perceptions because we have difficulty tolerating pain. We find it difficult, for instance, to acknowledge inner turmoil because we have learned to turn to outer reality in order to escape it. And for this very reason we are usually incapable of seeing what I have just described. This makes my task difficult: we are all shaped by our culture's dictates, which enjoin us to avoid the pain of inner chaos. Anxiety must be covered up, not confronted. In this way "sanity" becomes a very effective ruse used to conceal the pathology of a chaotic inner life. In the end we will not know ourselves that we are ill or desperate.

This constant covering up of our actual state of illness characterizes present-day life to a degree scarcely known before; in fact, it threatens the very survival of the human race. Ours is the sort of "sanity" Henry Miller describes as follows: we are so "sane" that if we were to pass ourselves on the road we would not recognize ourselves because the self confronting us would be so frightening.[6] We flee further and further from our inner desert, our inner emptiness, since we have no loving relationship to ourselves or others, and thus we flee at the same time from our own past.

In the absence of this dissociation, we react to what we do and what is done to us with feelings of pain and helplessness or joy and curiosity. As integral parts of our experience, these reactions are constantly being absorbed into our interior world, where they continue to exert their influence. They fuel our creativity, for they determine our receptivity to external stimuli. To the degree, however, that the value of these feelings is denied, our creativity is diminished. Cut off from our own inner life, we respond to the world only with externally imposed and preformed ideas and formulas. At this point we are close to becoming robots.

When pain, sorrow, and helplessness are denied because they are considered signs of weakness—because they are seen, for example, as unmanly, as effeminate sentimentality, as inappropriate to the ideal of masculine strength (an ideal also valid for women who base their concept of strength on the masculine model)—then our inner world becomes shut off and encapsulated from everyday life, sinking more and more into unconsciousness as a result. But it still remains the motor—even though unrecognized—of all our actions, thoughts, and feelings.

There are thus two basically different types of psychic structure. With the first, in which the inner world is accessible, people will be capable of creative responses to stimuli from the external world. This inner world can also exist on an unconscious level as long as it remains retrievable.

With the other type, when the inner world of feelings is closed off, it will be unaffected by the individual's interactions with the surrounding world. Or to be more precise: there will not be any true interaction at all. The extent of the resultant inner isolation is directly related to the degree of self-hatred, which is elicited in turn by the individual's active participation in his or her submission according to the dictates of a "reality" that demands the denial of autonomous feelings.

This continuing source of hatred intensifies a person's inner isolation as well as the chaos stemming from the lack of connection between the interior world and ongoing life. All this increases fear of the inner world and of its one day erupting into the open. Dissociation sparks more dissociation, and the fear of falling apart speeds up the individual's submersion in external reality, which teaches him or her to secure a place in a world devoted to power and domination.

It must be remembered that the encapsulation of the individual's inner sphere—its isolation from validating contact with the outer world—results in a lack of organization and integration. And this inner sphere is feared because destructiveness and self-hatred become its dominant elements.

Without organization the inner world remains in a state of turmoil, of chaos. The testimony of dreams substantiates this: the underlying mechanism of dreaming revolves around the retrieval of emotionally significant losses, be they wishes or unsatisfied needs. But in the case of dissociated people the wishes and unsatisfied needs are distorted or completely denied, which probably accounts for those patients who do not report dreams; this reflects the degree to which they are dissociated from the self.

Lack of integration gives rise to fear because of its potential explosiveness and especially because of the drive of human beings toward integration. Eric Aronson and Shelley Rosenbloom[7] have shown that infants only thirty days old express pain and discomfort when their previously whole and integrated perception of the mother is interrupted or broken off. The prerequisite for a whole human being is an inner life that receives rich stimulation from the outer world and can develop in an integrated exchange with it. This in turn is the precondition for becoming a "humane" person. On the other hand, the prerequisite for becoming evil is a much more complex development, one based on denial and destruction of the self.

The dissociative processes described here are very different from those we see in the case of schizophrenics, who attempt to remain in their inner world because they cannot tolerate the hypocrisy of the outer "real" one. They dissociate themselves from the outer world as a means of staying in touch with their own world of inner feelings and with the potential for autonomy contained in that world.

Conversely, a repression of despair and an inner imbalance—in other words, the dissociation of the inner life—distinguish those very people considered to have their feet firmly planted in reality. We think of them this way because our concept of "reality" is expressly tailored to fit this type of person and therefore is apparently validated by them again and again. For this reason it is such people whom we entrust with the power to determine our fate, although this is a responsibility they are thoroughly ill equipped to assume. But we do so because they embody our own fantasies of "realism" and strength.

The focus of this book, consequently, is upon the insidious nature of a "sanity" that hides the absence of a genuine self and simultaneously serves as a way of fleeing the inner chaos resulting from such an absence. For this dissociation of the inner world makes the development of a genuine self impossible.

The insanity masking itself as normality is fundamentally different from what is usually meant by that word; therefore, we need to reformulate the concept of insanity. Schizophrenia—the "recognizable" form of insanity—needs to be seen from a completely different perspective: namely, as the struggle against a much more portentous kind of insanity, one that has the semblance of normality. Here, again, we get a sense of the difficulty of my approach: we are all taken in by the outer appearance of normality, since, under the pressures of our upbringing, we have lost contact with what lies behind this facade.

The paradoxical aspect of present-day psychopathology is that, in the main, those people are classified as ill who are essentially trying to maintain contact with their own emotional world, not those who are trying to rid themselves of this contact. The illness of the former is all too often a reaction to the pressures on them not to recognize the contradictions and splits in the world of their experience. Their deeper malaise—which we do not see because our attention is completely diverted by their "crazy" behavior—is explained by the fact that schizophrenics are people who do not have the strength to preserve inner coherence when faced with society's contradictions and lies. Therefore, they cannot openly rebel or offer any resistance to societal pressures.

True integration of our experiences would also have to include their contradictory elements. Hypocritical standards would have to be recognized as such. A solicitude, for example, whose object is to keep another person dependent and thus under one's control, ought no longer to be seen as a "loving" solicitude, and yet most of us do see it in this light. That is the very reason why schizophrenics cannot identify with a world they regard as hypocritical and morally untrustworthy. Their feeling and thinking selves are estranged from each other, for to be otherwise would mean to submit to what they sense is inhumane: hatred, oppression, and control under the guise of love.

Schizophrenics' dissociation is their attempt to preserve

unity of feeling—in other words, their contact with the inner world—and their "insanity" is a protest against a tyrannically imposed "unity" that is actually not one at all. When, for instance, compassion becomes a way of pitying others in order to feel superior to them or simply to demean them, schizophrenics are unable to show empathy. They will laugh where we, the well-adjusted, expect kindness or concern as reactions. They are therefore diagnosed as having no relationship to reality and as being dissociated.

It is true that schizophrenics retreat into an inner space, but they do so because only there can they experience the reality of genuine feelings, which realism denies. Unfortunately, their attempt to maintain integration by cutting themselves off from the outer world leads to a diminishment of life and to psychic death. Such people try to divorce themselves by a process of nonidentification from a world they have experienced as hollow and false. That is why they end by not living in *our* reality.

To reach such a point, however, they must have experienced this reality with all its contradictions much more painfully than others. It is not that such people have a false perception of reality to begin with—originally they did know all about it—rather, for the very reason that they are so close to the truth, they find it impossible to go along with the pretense of a merely simulated wholeness. They become ill *because* of their effort to remain in contact with their inner life. It is the others, the "healthy" ones, who plunge into "normality" in order not to have to perceive what is going on inside. In a deep sense, then, schizophrenics are driven by their need to preserve wholeness, whereas the need of "normal" people is to keep things split apart.

For those who slip into the disguise of "normal" behavior because they cannot tolerate the tension caused by the contradiction between the reality imposed on them and their inner world, real feelings soon cease to exist. Instead, these people operate with *ideas* about feelings, not with *experi-*

ences of them. They display as their own those feelings that have been imposed on them and renounce their true feelings. The "saner" the image of the identity they have adopted the more successfully they will be able to perform this manipulation. And manipulation it is, for their goal is not self-expression; instead, they want to convince others that they act, think, and feel appropriately. These are the people whom I want to expose as the truly insane ones among us.

They endanger us all because they cannot face the chaos, the rage, and the emptiness inside them. In a world experienced as contradictory and painfully evil, schizophrenics preserve a central core of feelings that affirm the validity of genuine love; for those who trick their insanity, on the other hand, the pursuit of power becomes the only way to stave off the threat of inner chaos and dissolution. In order not to have to accept this inner emptiness as their own, they produce destruction and emptiness around them. The paradox of schizophrenics is that they try to protect their inner core by hiding it. This attempt is doomed to failure, for the self can live only through a vital exchange with the outside world; therefore, only too often schizophrenics pay for their effort with a total loss of all reason, logic, and communication. They do to themselves what the world has done to them. They make themselves unlovable in order to save others from having to feel guilty for their condition. The others, however, in order to avoid knowledge about their inner self, impose their "order" on their fellow men and women and thus their way of dealing with themselves.

While schizophrenics diminish themselves to avoid detection, "normal" people do the opposite: they diminish not themselves but reality by denying its contradictions and the fear this causes. Their lives turn into a defense of this diminishment and a denial of their inner fears. They cling to their diminished reality and insist that it represents the *whole* of experience. The self then willingly subscribes to a priori ideas about the nature of being instead of basing itself on the interactions between actual being and the surrounding world of which it is a part. Their consciousness thus does not reflect the integration of individual being and outer reality but the need to conquer this reality.

That is why a self obedient only to ideas rather than to the free play of feelings grounded in the experience of both joy and pain enslaves itself and becomes destructive. To the same extent to which we abandon ourselves to ideas, we mistake for feelings what are actually only notions of what we think we *should* feel. And, similarly, we believe we are thinking whereas our thought, in fact, is merely a quasilogical disguise for vengeful and destructive feelings. The "scientific" theories about "lives unfit for life" applied to the handicapped during the Third Reich are an extreme example of this.

This dilemma is caused by the capacity for dissociating thought and feeling inherent in the developmental process common to us all. As a result we see something as a function of our thoughts that actually is a function of our feelings and vice versa.

If we are prone to dissociate thought and feeling—that is, to distance ourselves from the roots of our feelings—the problem is that we will no longer be capable of an awareness of doing so. In keeping with our development we will strive to see ourselves not as we really are but as we think we ought to appear. Our image and our reality will not be isomorphic; that is, they will not correspond to each other. And if they do not correspond, this contradiction within our inner reality will be a constant source of fear, and the fear, in turn, will reinforce our dissociation. For example, our image of ourself as strong is contradicted by our sensitivity to another's pain because this sensitivity is equated with weakness. The contradiction threatens to cause us to break down, and our fear of breaking down causes us to "renounce" our feelings all the more.

This process can also be described differently: The notion

that domination equals strength and helplessness equals weakness exists to differing degrees, but it is present in all of us. We think this is a fundamental fact of our nature; yet the feelings we have about domination and helplessness are not in accord with those perfectly natural feelings we had during the initial period of our development when we were nourished and held in our mother's protective arms. If we later identify helplessness with weakness and domination with strength, such feelings are basically mere functions of thought processes, not of our intrinsic nature and experience. These thought processes are part of an already diminished form of reality, one marked by the inability to tolerate feelings. Thus, we again encounter a process involving dissociation.

It is primarily the inability to tolerate feelings that brings about dissociation between thought and feeling. Although this is considered a characteristic of schizophrenic behavior, it is true of us "normal" people and not of schizophrenics. In the latters' case, dissociation is an expression of the refusal to produce imposed and hypocritical feelings. For it is not that schizophrenics are incapable of tolerating real feelings of pain, sorrow, despair, or joy; they simply reject living with distortions of these feelings. But when "normal" men and women cannot tolerate helplessness, for instance, they need to seek relief in a "reality" that is contemptuous of such an experience and that denies its inherent potentiality as a source of genuine strength.

This reality, as a sign of strength, of necessity places particular value on the conquest of what lies beyond the borders of the immediate self. This results in a sense of illusory possession. Eugene O'Neill once referred to the United States as a moral failure because "[its] main idea is that everlasting game of trying to possess your own soul by the possession of something outside it, thereby losing your own soul and the thing outside of it, too."[8] Martti Siirala describes the same phenomenon on the level of the individual when he speaks of the "delusional possession of reality" as the central experience of the "adapted" person.[9]

Conquest and power will provide such people with confirmation that they are in contact with their feelings. But power and all its derivatives not only seem to give a sense of aliveness but also convey a false concept of human nature, which in turn alters human nature. For when individuals remain cut off from the inner self through "thinking" and submission to "thought's" dictates (the inner logic of thought permits no correction as long as genuine feelings and experiences are blocked out), not only will their autonomy be continually impaired but they will also become enraged and violent. The sole authentic element in such a state of spurious feeling is rage. But this rage will be disowned and will go unrecognized because the genuine feeling that would bring it to light is a threat to the ideology of artificial feeling.

Dissociation of consciousness is quite obviously an organizing principle in many personality structures. Blocking out our earliest perceptions not only makes it impossible for us to experience inner wholeness but also sets a pattern for dealing with feelings of helplessness and weakness. When we are no longer able to perceive the validity of our pain, we will also lack practice in coming to terms with helplessness, weakness, and impotence. Helplessness will then become an overwhelming threat against which we must arm ourselves with power. If this does not succeed, our experience of helplessness can very quickly be connected to a hallucinated event, which we will then interpret as the cause of our helplessness. A similar process takes place when people who previously have seemed normal suddenly exhibit surprising psychotic reactions accompanied by blind and destructive rage precisely when they have been wounded in their self-esteem. There have been countless examples of this in war and in cases of business failure.

We cannot live without trust, and we attain trust by experiencing a supportive affection. Without this affection, infants and small children can become apathetic and waste away or even die.[10] Even if the experience of being loved was there just once, in whatever form, our capacity for fantasy makes it possible for us to fill a subsequent void ourselves—with the goal of maintaining the life-supporting feeling of a bond with our mother. But if in constructing such fantasies we block out our painful experiences, then the self will rely on power and will rest on a diminished psychic base.

The American psychiatrist Harry Stack Sullivan once suggested that *one* positive experience suffices for a person to be convinced that he or she has only to find the "right thing" to do in order for the experience to be repeated.[11] Here fantasy obviously plays a crucial role by providing a life-supporting consolation no longer obtainable in reality. This is one of the ways people get by, for having to live with the loss of love is among the deepest forms of human despair. Children cannot live with the awareness that their needs and perceptions are rejected or denied unless their psychic structure is so altered that as a result they are able to deny their true needs.

To deny their inner needs, children must either completely or partially split them off. This dissociation involves a basic shift: in order not to be forced to perceive that father and mother are causing them pain, children will search in themselves for the cause of their despair. This tragedy, which leads to children's surrender of self, consists not only in the dissociation of their inner world but, beyond that, in the fact that—in order to maintain the life-giving bond with mother and father—they must see the lack of parental love as the result of a defect in themselves. They will therefore struggle to reverse parental disapproval and in the process continually try to find the fault in themselves. As a result they will shoulder the supposed guilt for the lack of love they sense and will begin a life of dreams and fantasies that fuel the need for power in order to overcome their "fault."

If children can succeed in adapting themselves to the

parameters set by the parental will and determined by the way their parents view them, then adaptation will become a strategy for survival. They will shunt aside their inner processes, disregard their own needs, expectations, and perceptions, and organize their lives on the basis of what lies outside the self. Along with this, their image of reality will shift in order to adapt to the ostensible coherence of a world of pseudofeelings. Consequently, the child's self will develop without any awareness of pain and death, yet at the same time will unwittingly be devoted to pain and death.

The central issue in individual psychological growth is the choice between two basic developmental directions: development toward the *outer* as opposed to the *inner* world. Development is directed toward the *inner* world if children receive the kind of love that enables them to experience helplessness without feeling all alone. If this is the case, helplessness will not be perceived as total abandonment or condemnation but as a state leading through pain and sorrow to new strength rather than to destruction. This sort of experience will produce a self that does not perceive helplessness as a deadly threat but as a possibility for new integration and new beginnings.

The other direction, the *outer* one, involves the dissociation of the experience of helplessness and the denial of the inner world in favor of acquiescence in an externally imposed order in which one's needs and perceptions are preformed, first by parents, later by school, society, and state. The horror of a helplessness that must be denied because it is experienced as a mortal danger continues in force, however, and becomes one of the motivating, although unconscious, factors in life. Inner and outer are of course dimensions of everyone's life, but they can become irreconcilable opposites. The extent of this dichotomy determines whether or not we will lead a fully responsible life, whether we will affirm ourselves and life, or whether we will devote ourselves to destructiveness and hatred of life, always placing the responsibility on others.

Classical psychoanalysis emphasizes the ubiquity of an inborn drive for self-gratification: this has both obscured the dissociation discussed here and helped to reinforce it. Such an emphasis makes us fear the child's aliveness, for psychoanalysis equates this with a supposedly innate proclivity for omnipotence and with an egoistic striving for limitless self-indulgence; in this way, it has positioned itself—probably unintentionally—on the side of arbitrary authority and against the child. This is paradoxical, yet it simply indicates how chained all of us are to the past, not excluding Freud, who, after all, placed the child at the center of all his thinking and lifework. Aarne Siirala has described the situation very well: "The therapeutic movement led by Freud creates connections with childhood, the ground of life's growth, the area from which man is estranged by his preoccupation with the effort to grasp and control reality in the framework of an industrial society."[12]

If, however, children's libidinous strivings for gratification are considered the main issue in their development, then their socialization will be viewed as a bulwark against "instinctual" drives rather than as a natural and self-generating process of growth. If instinct is pitted against social development, human nature will necessarily be *seen* as negative and destructive. Socialization regarded in this light merely reflects the established view of human relationships in terms of power relationships. In this view, the child wants to establish its power and omnipotence, but the adult must prevent this in the name of the "reality principle"; in order to teach children the correct relationship to reality, to help them adjust to it, adults must train them to "master" their drives, which means that children come to experience their needs as troublesome. They also learn that they are loved for successfully submitting to the parental will. For children, "mastering" something then means curtailing or "sublimating" their needs instead of integrating them with the world; it also means learning to mistrust their feelings. Psychoanalysis sees the essential psychic conflict as one between human drives and the demands of culture; accordingly, the "pleasure principle" has to be held in check by the "reality principle." Thus, successful social adjustment means the acceptance of culturally determined values that are considered to be basically at war with an unchanging human nature.

Freud showed great courage in reconnecting individuals to their own history, but he did this only in part; for as a child of his time, he shrank from the potential for human autonomy that might have come to light in the course of his analysis of childhood. That was the reason why he partially misinterpreted his clinical findings.[13] We can understand this better today if we proceed on the assumption that autonomous drives tend to conceal themselves in symptoms of pathological "otherness."

Naturally, Freud's patients displayed those forms of autoerotic fixation he described: for instance, they retired into social isolation, appeared to be completely self-absorbed, practiced incessant onanism. Freud thought that this behavior reflected the true drive structure of his patients as well as of humanity in general; he overlooked the fact that when infants are prevented from developing their personality through independent reactions to parental caretaking, they turn to dependency and the acting out of oral, anal, and genital fixations because these represent the sole possibility of self-expression. Children's fixation on "derived drives," which are artificial products of society, and their so-called power struggles to assert these "drives" do not reflect innate tendencies but rather their ability to confront parents with the very things they fear the most. Parental fears and expectations, not the instincts attributed to the child, are the determinants of this type of development.

From observing his patients, Freud arrived at the drive theory, which holds the "instincts" to be in essence socially negative; it would be much more convincing, however, to interpret these patients' symptoms as an expression of the human drive for autonomy "gone underground." Only when someone becomes the bad person or bad child that parents, school, and society secretly expect one to be—in other words, when one develops the very characteristics society tries to prevent one from developing by coercive means—can one feel outside the reach of authority. This is illustrated by what a patient once said to me: "You cannot touch *me* if I am as you wish."[14] By anticipating what the other person—in this case, the therapist—thought and desired, he himself remained "free." He did not have to invest himself in his actions since he did only what others expected of him. He was unreachable because he did not reveal his own will; this gave him the illusion of freedom. He had only one source of "satisfaction": a secret contempt for those who thought his "good" behavior was genuine. And this contempt, in turn, was directly nourished by his self-hatred, resulting from the daily surrender of his own potential to the will of others.

In this way true autonomy, the genuine need for intimacy, and the need to see the world with one's own eyes are relinquished in favor of a double dependency. The first part is as follows: "I am as helpless and dependent as you want me to be; therefore, you must keep on directing and correcting me, for I have no will of my own." This submissiveness, largely unverbalized and often completely unconscious, is simultaneously a form of revenge. One insists on being taken care of and on being dependent and insists on things staying this way. And there is another important element at play here: this is a way of never having to commit oneself, for one is only following orders. The meaning of life for people like this lies in obedience. We recall that war criminals frequently offered it as their excuse, which should once and for all awaken us to the true significance of every form of obedience, for behind this excuse all kinds of cruelty and murderous acts took place without their perpetrators having to

take responsibility for them. In a certain sense, the excuse
they offered was even correct: their own soul had nothing to
do with what happened; it was kept out of the reach of the
people being obeyed. *They* were the ones responsible. Under
these conditions, it is an easy matter for those who find
obedience to be their life's mission to switch masters.

Not to take responsibility for oneself is a major component of the Basic Lie. It conceals the original decision, *the* life
decision, namely: to resign oneself to submissiveness and
forfeit one's inner life in order to participate in power. This is
the crucial point at which people either do or do not accept
responsibility for themselves and vis-à-vis others. And this
point is obscured if, in order to explain betrayal of the self,
we simply specify the various forms of social repression and
see human existence solely in terms of a stimulus-response
mechanism, completely disregarding the possibility of autonomy.

The second aspect of this dependency becomes evident
when children justify their parents' worst fears, thus suc-
ceeding in evading parental demands yet at the same time
submitting to their parents' negative expectations, which are
for the most part unverbalized. In such situations, children
can feel vindictively righteous when they are told they are
disobedient; after all, they have paid strict attention to what
their parents "really" wanted—and now the parents reject
their children's resulting behavior!

This type of negative dependency produces the forms of
drive-fixation described by Freud. An illusory feeling of "independence" arises, a feeling that one is in control of oneself.
Masturbation, excessive eating, rejection of food, and other
extremely self-absorbed actions are behavior patterns that
suggest one is in charge of one's own stimulation. Such
patterns, generally labeled as compulsions, then take the
place of a genuine life. They nourish the illusion of independence and gloss over the actual ongoing state of dependency
against which the individual is desperately but vainly re-
belling.

The main trouble with psychoanalysis lies in its theory of the irreconcilability of human drives and the dictates of civilization. Here, it falls victim to the distortions of a culture that in the name of love forces people to give up their autonomy. In raising the results of this distortion—orality and dependency—to the level of basic drives, psychoanalysis obscures the cultural processes leading to psychological dissociation while at the same time strengthening them. Within the profession this has meant that many of its practitioners occupy themselves with the shadows of life rather than with life itself. Instead of helping their patients to find the strength to hold onto the truths they have discovered about their life situations, analysts cause their patients to become fixated on imaginary maladies.

If, however, our view is not clouded by these prejudices about childhood development, we will see that from birth on children quite obviously exhibit the capacity for an integrative, not a dissociative, approach. We do not find a need for omnipotence in infants and small children to begin with, unless rage and despair over inappropriate responses to their legitimate needs are interpreted as such. Only then do power struggles indeed ensue—because the adult expects them.

Infants are not motivated by dependency-producing autoerotic needs but by the search for those patterns of stimulation for which intimate exchanges with the mother during their life in the womb have prepared them. Their needs and expectations develop as a consequence of these earliest of interchanges[15] and make them look, from the very beginning, for new sources of stimulation rather than seek those gratifications—as psychoanalysis would have it—that perpetuate old stimulus situations. The major characteristic of these early patterns in the womb is their low intensity of stimulation (which, I should point out, on the biological level distinguish the processes that maintain life). Stimulation that is too intense leads to avoidance or interruption of movement toward the stimulus source. Most psychoanalytic theory is based on negative concepts of interaction (avoidance of unpleasant feelings and of danger, etc.) and thus fails as a universal theory of the human psyche.[16]

Where we do find compulsive patterns of self-stimulation—an extreme example is the shutting out of the external world that occurs in autism[17]—what we are dealing with is not an arrested normal development but a development that has taken the wrong direction. Withdrawal into self-stimulation and into forms of omnipotent behavior are expressions of *failure* in the development of autonomy, not expressions of an innate and universal human tendency from which people have to be saved by coercive socialization. The postulation of asocial drives as innate and universal obscures the fact that these drives are not determining factors in development but indications of problems in development. The instinctual-drive theory has prevented us from recognizing that the struggle for autonomy is the central issue in childhood development.

Autonomy as the integrating force in the development of self-directed personalities has nothing to do with ideas about one's own importance or uniqueness. These ideas are part of an ideology of the self that consciously or unconsciously subscribes to the principle that control and mastery over others is the source of self-esteem. Even rebels driven into militant opposition by their unfulfilled yearning for love remain ensnared in this ideology of the false self, for they incorrectly believe that autonomy means the "freedom" to display proof of their strength and superiority. It is irrelevant to them whether the *form* of this proof is in accord with current social norms or not; the crucial factor is to fulfill their urgent need for constant unrestrained self-assertion. And this produces a belligerence ill suited for affirming life.

Autonomy, as I see it, is a condition of integration in which the possibility of living in harmony with one's own needs and feelings is realized. What is meant here are not those feelings and needs artificially produced by the consumer society but those originating in the joy produced by a mother's love for the aliveness of her child or in the sorrow stemming from the lack of this love. Children's genuine reactions to the truth of their situation form the sole source of their autonomous development. Only when they do not have to deny their perceptions or feelings will they remain in contact with the inner and outer experiences that stimulate growth and be able to connect both kinds of experiences. Only then will they maintain contact with the roots of their feeling of aliveness; then, too, they will be able to assume responsibility for the direction in which this aliveness develops.

If this contact is severed, however, children will begin to conform exclusively to the "reality" imposed on them from outside. (It is the reality of power that led them to cut themselves off from their inner aliveness in the first place!) They will then nurse a self-hatred within that will drive them further and further into this dissociated form of orientation toward life.

I I

Self-Hatred as the Origin of Destructiveness

KLAUS BARBIE, THE feared Gestapo chief of Lyon, once made a significant admission. When he was questioned about his torture and murder of the French Resistance hero Jean Moulin, he said, "As I interrogated Jean Moulin, I felt that he was myself."[1] In other words, the more he recognized his own rejected self in Moulin, the more he had to hate and kill him—that is, himself.

This unusual and startling admission reveals that hatred originates in self-hatred. The murderer recognizes in his victim his own repudiated self, a self he has come to fear because it did not conform to his parents' needs for self-esteem, as a result of which the mother or father forced the child to submit to the parental will. A child treated in this way will later attempt to take revenge for such treatment: as an adult he will seek to be loved for inflicting pain on others while at the same time emphatically denying the true nature of what he is doing. If a man's development has taken this course, he will find his own suffering of long ago reactivated by his victim's plight; also, whatever remains of his own humanity will then be reawakened. That is why such men will invariably react to everything that recalls remnants of their own self with fierce contempt and with hatred, attempting in this way to silence the voice of the victim they so hate in themselves. Their connection to their own humanity is impaired because as a result of their childhood experience, which was closely bound up with a feeling of weakness, they interpreted their parents' exploitive love as "true" love.

Although I am speaking primarily of men here, of course women can also lose access to their feelings, as the terrible reports of female concentration camp guards have taught us. For in a culture like ours dominated by the ideology of male superiority, a woman's self-esteem will be based only too often on male criteria that deny the value of her feminine traits.

This unfortunate development in women is partially responsible for a mother's unconscious resentment of her own son, as well as for her overvaluation of him. This overvaluation increases the mother's need to dominate her son in order to use him to boost her self-esteem. My own findings and those of James R. Cameron have attempted to throw light on the complexities of this process. Cameron showed that it may take as long as three years after the birth of her son for a mother's hidden rejection to become apparent.[2] I was able to come to similar conclusions in my article about maternal rejection: the key to schizoid and overintellectual behavior in men probably lies in a culture's overvaluation of the male child and the mother's resulting ambivalence toward him. On the one hand, she rejects him because idealizing him denies her own womanly worth; on the other, her son is the source of her self-esteem in a world ruled by a male mythology. This explains why daughters are less frequently the objects of their mothers' ambitions, although they are not entirely spared these pressures. But if children, regardless of gender, become the object of an exploitive love disguised as "genuine" love, their approach to life will become fundamentally distorted. They will believe that it is not the person causing them pain who is at fault but that their own inner-most nature is "defective." They can then devote themselves to justifying this false love by insisting that those who op-press and hurt them really have their own good at heart. Concretely, this often manifests itself when an exploitive, manipulative, and domineering mother is defended as a good one. (Of course, the same defense can be made of a father with similar qualities.)

This Basic Lie accomplishes several things at once:

• It rejects true love, hating it because one's own inner self has been deemed defective. True love cannot be tolerated because if one has once accepted the blame for parental oppression, then one must deny everything that contradicts this belief in order not to be forced to hate one's parents. Henceforth, the false love that rewards "good" behavior becomes a person's exclusive goal. The attempt to win the approval of the very people who in fact negate us as human beings becomes the driving force in our life.

• In this same context of the Basic Lie, we find that duty takes the place of personal responsibility—a marked charac-teristic of our age. Here, abstract ideas can be substituted for the domineering parents whose approval had formerly been sought. Performance of duty becomes the impersonal motiva-tion for one's actions and gives an ersatz feeling of aliveness.

• The Basic Lie prevents us from admitting that we have surrendered to the will of others out of weakness, forfeiting our authenticity in order to participate in power. This partic-ipation as a strategy of survival and as a means of denying our sense of weakness in turn perpetuates the Basic Lie.

The Question of Duty

If social pressure makes performance of duty the main mo-tive in life, people's readiness to submit to the will of another is continually reinforced. In addition, whatever is left of the feeling of personal responsibility—and of the capacity for compassion—becomes more and more tenuous. Duty affords a welcome way to escape the sense of responsibility that might be awakened by compassion. If we opt for performance of duty, we avoid the pain our compassion might cause. People obsessed by the concept of duty are even prepared to die by faithfully performing it—and they think that by rendering allegiance to an abstract idea they are displaying responsibility.

Nowhere can we see the true nature of this "responsibility" better revealed than in the repeated claims of war criminals that they were "acting under orders." And this claim is inevitably followed by the statement, "They [the authorities] made me do it." This throws light on the true background of all performance of duty based on abstract concepts: the people in question typically avoid the sense of personal responsibility that would come from confronting their own standards. This is what Jakob Wassermann describes in *The Maurizius Case*: "Good and evil are not determined by the intercourse of people with one another, but entirely by a man's relations with himself."[3]

The focal point of this relationship with oneself is the experience of one's own pain and joy as well as empathy with the pain and joy of others. Whether this capacity exists or not depends upon the experiences the infant has had in physical proximity with the mother; in the truest sense of the word, the infant learns at its mother's breast "to touch the world with [its] searching mouth and [its] probing senses."[4] It is the immediacy of such feelings that communicates to the infant the pain and joy of being human.

We have all had this experience, but it has become distorted by societal pressures acting on us and causing us to move in an outward direction, away from the sources of our own feelings. If this externalization succeeds in divorcing us completely from our empathic capacities, we will also lose the ability to distinguish between duty and responsibility.

These will seem to us to be one and the same thing, and we will no longer notice that people appearing to act responsibly are in fact simply obeying a set of abstractions. One's position on the political spectrum plays no role here; a self organized according to the principle of power will always insist that it is behaving responsibly in terms of the political ideology dominant at the time. Yet the true nature of such an orientation will be revealed in all its externality when we observe how easily such "responsible" people can shrug off a whole set of "responsibilities" and shift direction as soon as the current power structure changes.

This phenomenon of a sudden shift to an opposite direction characterizing those devoted to a given set of rules, a leader, or a political ideology demonstrates very clearly what is involved in our usual concept of "identity"; it suggests that for many people identity and duty are in effect the same—for them, obedience and performance of duty constitute "identity." Wherever this is the case, we can be sure that no authentic inner self will be present. The history of Nazi Germany of course demonstrates this in an extremely drastic fashion.

Scarcely was the Nazi hegemony past when many people—without any awareness of the hypocrisy involved—switched from their loyalty to National Socialism to an allegiance to the new democratic or communistic norms. The lesson of Nazism is not only a history lesson in power politics, greed, megalomania, and evil; it also teaches us what men and women without any connection to their inner being are capable of. If we learn this lesson, it should help to protect us from a similar fate today, for such people are still among us. Instead of following political ideologies, nowadays they may follow, for example, the rules of success in the business world. In this context, they can change loyalties, that is, identities, much more frequently without even revealing their lack of a center. Indeed, flexibility in shifting loyalty—for instance, "corporate identity"—has become the test of adaptability and "realism." Thus, it has become more difficult to recognize the danger this kind of adaptability represents for humanity.

The Nazi era offers very concrete examples of this danger. Albert Speer, among other things Hitler's minister of armaments, clearly foreshadowed the modern type of successful manager so familiar to us now: obliging, a genius at sensing and manipulating the trend of the times, elegant, seemingly devoted to a high impersonal goal, amenable to anything— and therefore completely amoral and, despite his brilliant social exterior, without an inner core.

When Albert Speer was cross-examined by Robert H. Jackson, the American chief prosecutor at the Nuremberg trials, a man emerged who lacked the slightest sense of the contradictions between what is and what ought to be. During the war, he sent slave laborers into the arms factories without a thought for their rights or welfare. He was interested only in numbers. Although this man revealed a total lack of human emotions throughout his career, he made a great impression—as his memoirs of 1969 reveal—because of his urbanity, his sharp powers of observation, and his knowledge of *what one ought to feel.*[5] And here is the crucial point: the modern man of this type *knows* what feelings he is supposed to have, but does not *experience* the tension that would arise if he were actually to live with these feelings. For if this were the case, he would be confronted with the contradictions between the organizational necessities and goals he advocates and an empathic perception of the suffering of the human beings involved. Speer, who knew only too well what one ought to feel, was an embodiment of the soulless manager who understands how to convince the public what a feeling person he is. Even his former enemies believed this. For example, the *New York Times*, upon Speer's death, praised his "humanity."[6] Yet he was simply a man for whom *everything* was possible, thus even his complete turnabout in political allegiance after the collapse of the Third Reich.

In classifying such behavior as realistic, we lose sight of the underlying pathology: the absence of an authentic self and the ability to devote oneself, under the guise of organizational efficiency, to destruction and murder. A conservative German nobleman, Friedrich Reck-Malleczewen, who was murdered in Dachau in 1945, described this same Speer as a man who, "with that clean-cut expression of his," is "the epitome of this whole sickening, mechanical, little-boy-at-heart generation."[7] This conservative, whose resistance to German fascism came out of the inner core of a human being capable of compassion and, therefore, of moral stature, immediately recognized the soullessness of a conformist. It is precisely the Speers of this world, with their capacity for adjustment to "reality," who become the successful managers of this same reality.

Hans Frank, who at the age of thirty-nine became governor general of occupied Poland, is another example of today's successful man. He adjusted perfectly to every circumstance and always knew how to play the appropriate role—something he of course confused with acting with integrity. After a session of the Nuremberg trials, which he greeted as a "divinely ordained Day of Judgment" and as a necessary investigation of the recent reign of terror, he said to Gustave Gilbert, the American court psychologist: "I think the judges are really impressed when one of us speaks from his heart and doesn't try to dodge the responsibility. Don't you think so? I was really gratified at the way they were impressed by my sincerity."[8]

This clearly reflects a person who, in keeping with the nature of artificial feelings, can actually produce them like an actor. He was, as Dr. Gilbert put it, "the showman of his conscience,"[9] who felt neither shame nor sorrow nor guilt for his deeds but merely played the role his idea of conscience dictated to him. This man presented his audience with a dramatization of shame, not with a genuine experience of it.

Frank also inadvertently presents us with evidence that

reversals of identity are a feature of externally derived selves. In further conversations with Gilbert, he spoke of his "surrender" to Hitler. "Those three days after Hitler committed suicide were decisive—the turning point in my life. After he had led us on and set the whole world in motion, he simply disappeared—deserted us, and left us to take the blame for everything that had happened. . . ." After Frank had shifted his obedience to the democratic victors, he explained his surrender to Hitler as follows: "You know, the people are really feminine . . . so emotional, so fickle, so dependent on mood and environment, so suggestible . . . so ready to obey . . . not merely obedience, surrender, like a woman."[10]

His contempt for women of course merely reflects the deeper contempt he had for his own self. Yet since he had no access to his inner self, he was not aware of this, and, therefore, he was caught in a round of repeated surrenders. This is an example of the reversibility of identity of which I'm speaking, again demonstrated at the Nuremberg trials, during which Frank was so intent on exhibiting his remorse. A film of Hitler was shown in the courtroom—and once again Frank surrendered: He told Gilbert, "When I saw him in that film in court, I was swept along again for a moment in spite of myself. I am such a responsive individual. . . . For a moment you are intoxicated . . . but then it passes—you open your hand, and it is empty—utterly empty."[11]

The identity reversal of this man with his outer-directed self reveals still more about such men and their lack of genuine feelings. In one of his diaries covering the period before the defeat of German fascism, Frank reports on a meeting in Cracow, Poland, at which he said: "Gentlemen, I must ask you to rid yourselves of all feeling of pity. We must annihilate the Jews, wherever we find them and wherever it is possible. . . ."[12] When he was later asked how he had been able to write with such equanimity and apparent delight of the mass murder and extermination carried out under his

command, he answered: "I don't know. I can hardly understand it myself."[13] At that point, he was probably even
speaking the truth; an outer-directed self simply obeys the
powers of the moment. As soon as this obedience shifts, as in
Frank's case to the democratic victors, such a person is
incapable of understanding his previous self, for if he were to
attempt to understand, he would be facing an inner void.
Frank could tell us that he felt empty, but he did not have the
inner strength to face the pain and suffering a real act of self-
confrontation demands. He called himself a "responsive"
individual, but this kind of responsiveness is merely the quest
for an outer identity, the quest for something to surrender to
in order to avoid responsibility.

These examples force us to reexamine the concept of identity. Commonly, it is understood as the basic constellation of
personality traits unique to an individual and setting her or
him apart from others. Yet an identity based only on identifying with others may be nothing more than a set of duties
surrendered to in order to escape one's own identity. The
resultant identity constitutes a betrayal of the self, a settling
for a lie about the self, which then intensifies one's inner
emptiness and hatred.

The nature of this inner emptiness tends to escape our
notice precisely because those people affected by it are so
well aware of how they ought to behave. They are experts in
appearing to be feeling human beings. If we are not alert and
fail to see that they sense no moral tension between what is
and what ought to be, we will take their appearance for
reality and attribute genuine human traits to them. This
occurs so frequently because our civilization considers inner
"tension" of this kind to be illness.

Adolf Eichmann best illustrates the absurdity of such an
"identity." Here was a man who at his trial in Jerusalem
could say of his participation in "the Final Solution," "I must
point out that I do not consider myself guilty from the legal
point of view," but he could also say, "I regard the murder,

the extermination of the Jews as one of the most hideous crimes in the history of mankind."[14] This man who had been responsible for the death of millions was able to quibble in this fashion about details of his historical image. Yet in the presence of the power his Argentinian captors represented, when he had to move his bowels, after having sat down on the toilet, he obediently asked his guard, "May I do it now?"[15] In performing one of the most private bodily functions, he surrendered his will, yet at the same time he quibbled at his trial about aspects of his external identity.

Hannah Arendt's famous formulation "the banality of evil"[16] is not quite accurate. Rather, evil has its roots in the perversion of human potential, in people without true selves. Arendt criticized the Eichmann trial because it attempted to explain the defendant's actions by his evil character. She countered by claiming that Eichmann was simply a deadly normal bureaucrat who did not know what he was doing. She failed to see in him the ultimate perversion of our time: that people can give the appearance of having feelings when in fact they have none.

Identity, Self-Hatred, and Criminality

Self-hatred is not only a result of the surrender of the self; once in place, it serves as a continuing reinforcement of such self-betrayal. The greater the degree of submission, the less likely the awareness of self-hatred. People who forgo a true self and who are unable to find an ideology of duty can often become open criminals. This type of criminal behavior, which openly violates society's laws, must be distinguished from the less overt variety that commits injustice in the guise of legality. Both have internalized power as the one valid reality, but the open criminal hates the "love" that is at the root of his development, and he opposes its idealization. He does not accept the dominant ideology of duty, does not identify with it, and thus does not behave in accordance with society's expectations. On the other hand, criminal activity that hides behind the mask of an official identity requires an authoritarian ideology to conceal its murderousness from itself.

Klaus Barbie is a prime example of an official murderer. He was twenty when his father, a chronic and violent drunkard, died; up to that time Klaus had been a devout Catholic, remembered by the inhabitants of his native city of Trier as a boy of mild temperament who had done relief work among the poor. After his father's death, he joined the Hitler Youth and discarded his pious identity for a devious and vengeful one. His youthful "devotion" to Christian charity and his sense of mission vis-à-vis the destitute turned into a neo-pagan militancy that subscribed to the doctrine that the weak have no right to exist.[17]

Barbie began his career by informing on fellow members of the Catholic youth organization to which he belonged; then, at age twenty-two he became a member of the security branch of the SS. Clearly, he did not find it difficult to defend the weak one day and scorn them the next. It is not simply that the ability to reverse identities reflects the lack of an authentic self but also that a lack of authenticity works hand in hand with a capacity for changing identity to breed destructiveness. One can be devoted to charitable activities and at the same time be filled with hatred, for obeying the rules of a given social group can arise simply from the need to partake in power. Submission to Christian rules, as in Barbie's case, can be motivated solely by a need to *overcome* one's sense of helplessness, not to *live* with it. And that is why one hates oneself.

This problem of obedience still haunts all those Germans today who, with the end of the war and the Nazi state in 1945, so easily switched their allegiance from fascism to democracy. Their true self was never really involved—neither before nor after 1945, and, therefore, their inner malaise has never ceased. In fact, since the war's end this malaise has become even worse than it was during Hitler's time, because it was easier then to project inner hatred onto outer objects behind the mask of the fascist ideology of virtue and greatness. A "democratic" identity based, like the authoritarian one, on obedience rather than on a sense of personal responsibility will remain the helpless prey of accumulated hatred and resentment, for it cannot as easily find scapegoats for the discharge of these feelings.

One of the most important features of every self-betrayal is the hope not for love but for finding the key to the power by means of which one can overcome what is felt to be insufferable inadequacy (that is, helplessness). People for whom this key lies in identification with the power oppressing them believe they can free themselves from their weakness by means of their participation in power. Others hope to find liberation from their helplessness in "success." In Barbie's case, obedience to the norms of his childhood social milieu was connected with his mother's ambitions for his education and career.

As long as the social framework within which obedience and self-betrayal develop remains intact, its promises retain their validity, and inner hatred need not emerge into the open. But when this framework collapses—when, for example, economic conditions make a promised participation in power impossible for many—then the subliminal hatred toward others of people without a self will surface.

Alexander and Margarete Mitscherlich's analysis of Germany's postwar malaise, *The Inability to Mourn*, is—despite its brilliance and profundity—inadequate. The authors diagnose an inability to mourn as basic to German problems after the Second World War, and they attribute this to a narcissistic wound.[18] But how can people mourn if their identity is marked by an absence of authenticity? If a genuine self is absent, so are authentic feelings; therefore, genuine mourning is impossible. The concept of narcissism, with its notion of an injury to "the ego's cathexis," obscures the actual situation in which a lie about love has become the fulcrum of personality organization. What needs to be recognized is that the problem lies in the lack of an authentic self; narcissism is merely a symptom of this condition, not its cause. In order to deal with a deficit in a patient's feelings, therapists must first realize the person before them is completely *incapable* of feeling. To bring such people back to what they rejected about themselves so long ago means to accompany them on a journey of self-confrontation so painful that suicide, an outbreak of psychosis, or some other dire result may ensue. Any other approach is empty talk with which therapists seek to conceal their own helplessness.

When the collapse of a social framework liberates subliminal hatred, those affected usually embark on a search for a new identity, for a new set of rules—rarely a search for the genuine self. For Klaus Barbie, his world collapsed when his father's death put an end to his hopes of attending a university; thus, a number of careers were closed to him. It was at this point that he turned against his Catholic faith.

The degree to which he despised his earlier ideals is illustrated by his subsequent history. When he fled Europe after the war (with the aid of U.S. counterintelligence), of all the possible aliases he might have chosen he took the name Altmann. Altmann had been the chief rabbi of Barbie's native city. It was Barbie who had him tracked down in Amsterdam in 1942 and deported to an extermination camp. Rabbi Altmann had been known for his wisdom and gentleness. It was this man's identity Barbie chose for his flight to Bolivia, where he lived under this name until his extradition to France in 1983! That Barbie assumed an identity whose hallmark was love must be seen both as an act of arrogation and as one of mockery. In this way he mocked love—just as he had had to kill the voice of humanity in himself when he murdered the French Resistance fighter Jean Moulin.

If Klaus Barbie had been loved for himself as a child, perhaps the world would have experienced one less horror.

To be sure, his mother was not cruel to him in the usual sense of the word. She is described as fair-minded and moderate—in contrast to his father—and at the center of her son's affections throughout her life. But that this affection could not have been what it appeared to be is made clear by Barbie's especially fiendish behavior toward women prisoners, whom he treated with extreme sadism, flirting with them and flattering them even while degrading and torturing them. This mockery of women betrays the degree of his underlying hatred for womanhood itself. The Basic Lie about love must have played a particularly devastating part in this man's "adjustment," which resulted in his defense of his mother as the "good" mother, whereas in reality he had experienced her as the "bad" one. He subsequently poured out his subliminal hatred against those women whom he perceived as embodying the potential for genuine love.

When children learn that love can be won only through maneuvers of compliance, they exchange the hope of being loved for themselves for the hope of power. And if children settle for this exchange, they will necessarily feel contempt both for themselves and their mothers. But this contempt and the resultant hatred will be denied, for an honest recognition of the situation would mean confronting their own submission and the motivation behind it: namely, the bartering away of their need for true love in return for the promise of power.

For a male who has made such an exchange, both as a boy and later as a man, a pure and inviolable love will become the object of destructive desire. Jakob Wassermann probably comes closest to describing the inner processes in murderers like Barbie in his fictional portrait of the thief and killer Niels Heinrich Engelschall in the novel *The World's Illusion*. Niels Heinrich's terrible emptiness and wild rage are revealed in the author's description of him as believing "there were no real things in the world except stench and misery and avarice and greed and treachery and malevolence and lust." The world is seen here only in terms of power, a power bereft of all possibility of an alleviating love. Wassermann goes on to describe him as thinking that the world "was a loathsome thing and had to be destroyed. And any one who had come to see that, must take the last step, the very last, to the place where despair and contempt are self-throttled, where you could go no further, where you heard the Angel of the Last Day beating at the dull walls of the flesh, whither neither the light penetrated nor the darkness, but where one was alone with one's rage and could feel oneself utterly, and heighten that self and take something sacred and smash it into bits. That was it, that! To take something holy, something pure, and become master of it and grind it to the earth and stamp it out."[19]

Wassermann presents here what Barbie revealed in the interview quoted at the beginning of this chapter and what criminals of his type tend to camouflage with ideological phrases. The true criminal is more honest and exhibits more clearly what both have in common: emptiness and rage. Both torture to death what is sacred—in the case of Niels Heinrich a woman who is pure in her beliefs. Both are sustained by their rage against love, against the pristine purity of the feelings they had as children. Only hatred and destructiveness give them a feeling of aliveness. Only through rage and murderousness can they attain a feeling of wholeness and a heightened sense of self.

All this may begin with nothing more than a mother's promise to her child that he or she will have great importance for her if the child does what the mother wants. A mother does not need to express this directly; the message is usually delivered in subtle, nonverbal ways. To make children sense they are more important than anyone else (including their fathers) is the surest way to give them the feeling that they possess an importance they cannot possibly have. The promise of such power obscures for the child both the mother's exploitive behavior and the child's own helplessness. Herein lies the seductiveness of power as an antidote to the child's despair and pain. Once this interaction begins, the stage is set for children to shut off their access to pain and sorrow, which could otherwise have constituted the source of future receptivity and integration.

Children who experience pain at not being accepted for what they are will not always be directly seduced by power. Self-hatred can also arise if they are given a sense of inferiority and instilled with a fear of self-realization. If this is the case, however, the possibility remains that their suffering and its source will become conscious. Such people will not necessarily seek out a power-oriented career.

But those people whose destructiveness is our concern here are human beings who at the end of their misdirected development are capable of obedience but not conviction. Their obedience fuels their self-hatred and destructiveness. This hatred is the product of their socialization, not of an innate drive. Freud was correct in observing that there is a destructive element in all people, but by positing this as a universal instinct he helped to obscure its origin in self-hatred.

Everything that diminishes the unity of development also diminishes the human capacity for aliveness and responsibility. With the loss of wholeness comes a constant inner unrest. Pain and suffering are dismissed as weakness rather than recognized as meaningful human reactions. Power as the means of compensating for feelings of helplessness and weakness becomes the way to undo the results of self-engendered dependency. And because power arrogates to itself the right to determine what is reality, addiction to power is equated with "realism." Yet this can lead to nothing but the idealization of death.

I I I

The Covert Cult of Death

ALL OF US have experienced the shelter of life in the womb and the subsequent emergence into a social world with its alternating feelings of security and despair. All of us are capable of giving up the unity of our experience by isolating aspects of this experience. This happens because the pain and distress caused by nonrecognition and false love are too great. The degree and frequency of the resulting dissociation determine whether the individual will become more or less strongly outer directed.

Thus, a turning point in human development appears very early. It is *as if* a child needs to decide either to maintain contact with its inner life and preserve its potential for autonomy or cut itself off increasingly from its inner experience. If this dissociation is radical, the person in question will no longer be reachable by those who are in touch with their inner selves.

Communality among human beings ceases at that point where those without access to their own pain and despair lose their empathic perceptiveness. What subsequently remains in common is only what lies outside the sphere of the inner life, and this depends in turn upon experiences of power that have become a part of the individual's personality structure. As a result, two personality types emerge, with differing capacities for experiencing a common world: this explains why two completely divergent views of "reality" exist, one based on an integrated inner life in harmony with outer reality, the other dominated by outer-directedness. Naturally, there are numerous overlaps. What interests us here is the fact that those people most cut off from their inner life, who, to maintain their personality structure, are more and more subject to direction from the outside, are also the most active in promoting their "reality." This forces their opposites to take the defensive, and, consequently, there is little room left for tolerance between the two groups.

What separates these opposite views of reality in everyday life becomes especially clear under the extreme conditions of warfare. Wilhelm Kütemeyer gives an example of this in his study of Europe's illness of soul after the Second World War when he describes a patient who had killed during the war without being conscious of the murderousness of his deeds:

A short time ago a patient came to me complaining that he was no longer able to go on with his daily work. He was continually haunted by scenes that had taken place on a sinking steamship. Toward the end of the war the ship—unaccompanied on the high seas, overloaded beyond its capacity with twenty thousand passengers divided between soldiers and fleeing civilians—was torpedoed by an enemy submarine shortly after nightfall. Terrible scenes ensued. The lights went out, the few lifeboats capsized under the weight of the people crowding into them. The hastily set up emergency lighting system was immediately put out of commission again by frantic women. My patient, an officer, who was lying wounded below deck, tried, along with another wounded comrade, to restore order by shooting a number of these women. They used a pistol at close range. He cannot shake off the memories of this incident, in which the women, some of them with babies in their arms, fell to the ground with that

slightly astonished look of sadness on their faces that was
already indelibly imprinted on his mind from the executions
of comrades he had been ordered to carry out. He reproaches
himself particularly for not having felt anything during the
entire episode except the slightly nervous anticipation of that
strange expression on the faces of the women he shot; aside
from that he had felt no emotion or excitement at all. He was
one of the approximately two hundred people to be rescued,
due to the fact that as a pilot he was wearing a life jacket with
phosphorescent markings. This made him visible in the dark
to crew members of a torpedo boat, which then picked him up
in an unconscious state.[1]

This story shows a man who, as already stated, killed
without being aware of the murderous nature of his actions.
In further descriptions, Kütemeyer fills in the portrait of a
dissociated person. The patient's indifference toward dread-
ful events came to light when he talked about his childhood.
When he was six years old, he had seen a friend die of
diphtheria, and he described watching with curiosity as the
boy suffocated before his eyes; it was as if he were interested
only in adding to his knowledge. Then his father, to whom
he had been especially attached, also died. At the funeral he
was conscious merely of his own presence, not of any inner
involvement. Nor did he have any sense of grief until half a
year later. Only then did his feelings break through.

After Kütemeyer had summoned forth these memories
from his patient, he asked him how he had felt under artillery
fire or during bombardments. The unequivocal answer:
"Good, very good." This patient never felt better than in
such situations, for that was when he was really in his
element—when he could be active, rather than forced to be
immobile and passive. In general, he felt particularly attracted to catastrophic situations, in civilian life as well. "For
example, automobile accidents had an irresistible, magnetic
attraction for him. And here, too, to be able to help the
victims made his day. Otherwise, he never felt closer to
people, even those he was closest to, than after they had

died—of course, only after a period marked by absence of emotion."[2]

This man had obviously lived outside his feelings since childhood. Instead of being compassionate, he was merely curious in an objective way and was fascinated by observation for its own sake. When we look more closely, we notice that the objects of his observation were death and destruction. The victims were what interested him; the growing number of casualties on the battlefield sustained him. His demeanor as a boy had revealed nothing but good manners and healthy ambition, yet as an adult he sought out encounters with death under the guise of following orders and performing duty.

Kütemeyer asks: "Can there, for example, be a more fortunate situation for people like this than a war?" They never dodge danger and are always to be found where it is greatest: "But let it be noted: not out of a willingness for self-sacrifice, but because they never . . . feel so well on this earth as when in danger like this."[3] Here lies the crucial point: death and destruction give meaning and solidity to their lives. Under the guise of discipline and scientific curiosity, such people's underlying hatred passes for "objectivity." On the sinking ship, this approach culminated in the insane attempt to enforce discipline where discipline had become meaningless.

Admittedly, this man showed "feelings," since he so often and willingly hastened to the aid of accident victims, yet that only confirms my point about the artificial nature of these feelings. His helpful behavior was not rooted in compassion but was based on the image he had of himself as a compassionate person. How else can we explain the fact that he felt no compassion on the ship as he calmly shot down women with babies in their arms? Our confusion about this behavior will be dispelled if we consider that outer-directed people are often playacting when they display feelings. The desire to present the correct image is what motivates them to perform apparently compassionate deeds.

The audience before which one performs may be actual or

only imagined. In the latter case, it is an internalized public, whose origins go back to the father and mother, for whom one has wanted to appear "correct." Feelings that have taken this path of development arise from the need to please but also to feel pleased about oneself for "correct" and "proper" behavior. The major concern is to be—or at least appear— agreeable; it is in this connection that "feelings" for others are displayed, not because of any actual empathic perceptiveness. This is true narcissism, a condition produced by a culture that so readily gives its approval for "nice" behavior.

In cases like this, public-spiritedness and compassion, although merely simulated, are easily taken for genuine feelings. The playactors consider their performance real and genuine, since correct behavior is the basis for their self-love. And this way of acting will continually reinforce their lifelong self-deceit, serving at the same time to assuage the ever-present doubts stemming from their early betrayal of self. For this reason, any challenge to their "correct" behavior arouses a violent response. Their violence is a sign of the reservoir of hatred people without a true center harbor within themselves as well as of that underlying self-contempt and the sense of weakness that is the lot of those who have accepted the promise of power as a substitute for the love they really crave.

This explains why Kütemeyer's patient felt closest to someone dead! There, at least, his insufficiency and that of people like him would never be challenged. If death is what offers the greatest safety to such a man, then that is what he longs for. It is no accident that ideologies that express the deepest contempt for compassion and pay the greatest homage to the male mythology of strength and heroism have been and continue to be the fascist ones. And every one of them glorifies death. This is the reason they find emotional support among so many people, including even those intellectually opposed to them. These movements touch upon a tendency in many of us to be fascinated with death as heroic redeemer, for it liberates us from gnawing doubts about our insufficiencies. This is true for men as well as for women whose selves are based on the mythology of maleness. That is why it is so easy for fascists to win over both men and women to their destructive goals. If this need for deliverance had not already been present, fascism could never have been so successful.

The longing for death is a component of a personality structure that is without authenticity. The tradition of tragic love stories in which death plays the role of deliverer attests to its all-pervasiveness. Romeo and Juliet may serve as examples here: Can it be that their plight moves us not only because we pity them but because their fate is dimly sought by the audience too? For why, we must ask, are so many murders committed in the name of love? Do lovers, husbands, and wives kill each other because they love each other so much? Perhaps the infatuation with love has little to do with love itself but is a way of insisting upon being loved by another person in order to escape one's own inner struggles. And these struggles have to do with the inability truly to love oneself. If our original love for our own nature has been supplanted by narcissistic self-love based on approval from outside, then we cannot dare to love our true self.

Thus, we seek to love our self in another person, specifically in one whom we find "worthy" of our love. In this way, however, we lose ourselves *and* the other person. Sometimes we even reach the point of trying to kill this self—by actually killing the other person. For, in fact, it is the self, which we had originally surrendered, that we think we have recovered in another person, but then—sobered by reality—lose once again. At this juncture, our hatred for our betrayed self gets the upper hand—and therefore we kill out of "love."

A covert longing for death is all around us. It is not only the loss of self that is responsible for this but also the fact that the loss has come about with one's own collaboration. (The instrumental role here of the mother—if she is trapped in the mythology of maleness—will be discussed in subsequent chapters.) The seeking of death is no more widespread today than it was in earlier times; it is simply that the means of wreaking total destruction have increased enormously, as has concealment of the fact that death is the aim of our actions. Even Hitler and his cohorts felt it necessary to pay lip service to life.

During the Third Reich, there were instigators of mass murder who did not hesitate to speak of the moral difficulty of acts of murder! Heinrich Himmler addressed a gathering of SS generals at Posen in October 1943 regarding the extermination of the Jews as follows: "Most of *you* must know what it means when a hundred corpses are lying side by side, or five hundred or a thousand. To have stuck it out and at the same time (apart from exceptions caused by human weakness) to have remained decent fellows, that is what has made us so hard."[4] In Himmler's pose of being horrified at his own actions, the awareness of doing something horrible is nevertheless present, but the main emphasis has been shifted to a feeling of self-pity that prevents the emergence of other emotions. This is central to the nature of feelings displayed for public effect: one pities oneself in order to avoid feeling empathy but also in order to feel more justified in attacking those who question the Basic Lie.

On another occasion, in May 1944, Himmler spoke before a conference of Nazi Gauleiters about the difficulty of carrying out the extermination of the Jewish people: "I am talking to you within these four walls and you must listen to what I have to say and let it go no further. All of us have asked ourselves: what about the women and children? I have decided that this too requires a clear answer. I did not consider that I should be justified in getting rid of the men—in having them put to death, in other words—only to allow their children to grow up to avenge themselves on our sons and grandsons. We have to make up our minds, hard though it may be, that this race must be wiped off the face of the earth."[5] To organize this, he continued, was the most difficult task yet, but no one had suffered any damage in mind or soul on the narrow path between the Scylla and Charybdis of becoming either a heartless ruffian without any feelings for human life or a weakling with a nervous breakdown. Men like Himmler know what feelings one ought to have and thus allege feelings that are wholly contradicted by their behavior. Speeches such as these were supposed to give the impression that the murderers in question had a choice between becoming either "heartless ruffians" or "weaklings." The language was intended to confuse those who still had some traces of genuine feelings left. By subtly shifting the question from horror to an idealization of the one committing it, Himmler introduced the hidden weapon of guilt in case anyone should waver. The "real" question then becomes whether one has the "will" to overcome inner torment. This was meant to make the members of Himmler's audience eager to display manly strength and renounce any humane feelings they might still have.

We tend to consider guilt feelings to be typical of a humane person; this view is entirely unjustifiable, however. A genuine consciousness of guilt involves a reawakening of empathic sensitivity and is characterized by an inner sense of shame along with the attempt to right past wrongs. What we generally call guilt is at the most contrition—an outer-directed reaction of submission that is supposed to win the favor of the authorities. This merely keeps in motion the cycle that produced destructiveness in the first place; it does not create the conditions for real change. Change is possible only for those people who are truly horrified at what they have done as a result of their false identity and are prepared to face the pain this causes. Only in a development that does *not* lead to autonomy do guilt feelings play an important role. They are the primary weapon against autonomy. For instance, if children do not fulfill parental demands for "correct" behavior, their self-esteem will suffer; then, as adults, guilt feelings become part of the force driving them further and further away from their true selves. Their own feelings will be a source of guilt. Guilt feelings serve primarily to obscure the origins of people's destructive rage. At the same time, they reintroduce an old mechanism: instilling feelings of guilt in their children is a favorite strategy used by parents to manipulate them. If we therefore attribute genuine feelings to people with guilt feelings, we shall for the most part be wrong, seeing autonomy and humaneness where they often do not exist.

We can overcome the attraction exerted by death and destruction only if we truly experience another person's pain—not our own self-pity. If our potential for this is still present, our attitudes and actions can change, regardless of external danger. The Swiss journalist Ernst von Schenck cites the case of a German soldier during the Second World War that is relevant here. This man was ordered to kill a Russian soldier who had just surrendered; in the immediacy of the encounter, however, the Russian was not merely an abstract enemy but a human being who, like his captor, felt fear and desperation. As a result, the German soldier could not kill him. What is more, the moment he experienced his inner opposition to the order to kill the Russian, he recognized the nature of his self-surrender to the Nazi mythology. Simultaneously, with this return to his own humanity, there awakened in him an active resistance to the Nazi regime.[6]

It is at such turning points that we learn something about genuine feelings. They stem from our primary experiences of pain and joy rooted in early emotional exchanges with our mothers. The immediacy of a human situation will often cause the wall of abstractions separating us from our empathic potential to crumble—proof that the inner world, for all its roots in the past, is a present reality and also a visible sign that most, if not all, people can reclaim a portion of their buried humanity. If a reawakening of humanity does occur, the person experiencing it cannot but act accordingly. If such a breakthrough does not take place, it is a measure of people's degree of dissociation from their inner world and of their lack of strength to face the truth about themselves.

An occurrence of a breakthrough to humanity is illustrated by the story of David B. Johnson, an American soldier in the Vietnam War. A seven-year-old Vietnamese girl suddenly appeared in his unit, holding in each hand a grenade with the pin pulled out. "I was the only armed man within reach. At the third order [of an officer] I obeyed and killed her." That and another similar incident on the same day changed his whole life. "After that the horror of what I saw day after day just built up inside of me. . . ." David had been brought up on the very kinds of abstractions that smother one's compassion and capacity to perceive pain and suffering. He told a reporter in Paris in 1971 that he had joined the army as a volunteer, supporting it heart and soul. His ideological background was the arch-conservative John Birch Society, "and I sincerely believed all that stuff about defending the free world against communism." He was wounded in Vietnam and returned to a hospital in the United States. While convalescing he went AWOL in order to engage in antiwar activity, but was caught. "I'll tell you," he said to the reporter, "just how pro-American [that is, reactionary] my family is. After I split from jail, I went home and my mother gave me two hours to get out or she was going to call the police."[7]

There can be no awareness of conflict between ideology and feeling when their irreconcilability threatens individuals with the collapse of their external and ungenuine self. If real feelings surface, they will be accompanied by fear of chaos and insanity. These people will need to cling more than ever to their chosen "reality." Yet even here we can usually find remnants of their original self. Few people can fully evade responsibility for another's pain, unless their own empathy never had an opportunity to develop. And since our empathic potential apparently already starts developing in the womb, we have all had this opportunity. Psychosomatic symptoms are often the result of withheld empathy. Of course, such symptoms do not make us better human beings, but they are nevertheless evidence that we start out with the potential for human feelings. Even Heinrich Himmler suffered from stomach cramps when he was organizing the extermination of the Jews, according to the report of his Finnish masseur.[8] This type of reaction has been confirmed experimentally, as in the famous Milgram experiment, during which subjects were told to inflict pain on another human being on command. Although most subjects obeyed the order of the experiment's director, they experienced in the process psychosomatic symptoms such as trembling, perspiring, or even cramps.[9]

Of the many illnesses reported among guards in the extermination camps of the Third Reich, most were nothing other than reactions to their inner denial of the sufferings of others. After an especially gruesome execution of eighty men near the crematorium in Auschwitz, SS Sergeant Mussfeld underwent a physical examination on account of high blood pressure. When told his pressure was high because of what he had just done, he shouted: "Your diagnosis is wrong. It doesn't bother me to kill a hundred men any more than it does to kill five. If I'm upset, it's only because I drink too much."[10] Alcohol was, of course, the most common way for these men to numb themselves; others intensified their cruelty or—also not uncommonly—committed suicide.

Why is it so difficult for us to recognize that people are devoted to death, and to understand the nature of this devotion? We are confused, as already stated, by feelings that are displayed for effect. We have been so pressured into conformity that we are ashamed of being receptive to the suffering of other people. Yet empathy is originally our primary means of interpersonal communication; its primacy, as well as its continuing existence in everyone, is attested to whenever superimposed ways of perceiving—the culturally learned ways—are impaired or disappear: for example, when we are exhausted or when the nerve centers of the brain involved with the socialization process are damaged.

A recent investigation of prosopagnosia has direct bearing here. In this condition, bilateral damage to the mesial occipitotemporal cortices of the brain's visual system makes it impossible to recognize familiar faces. Even after patients recognize people they know by their voices or by some other cue, "their physiognomies remain meaningless." Thus, the illness is marked by a complete lack of cognitive memory.

In the study in question, the investigators were interested not only in the patients' verbal reports but also in the possibility of covert processes that might be occurring without the patients' awareness. With the help of an electrodermatogram, they measured skin conductance response to processes of the autonomous nervous system—that part of our nervous system that transmits empathic feelings. Thus, this study is particularly relevant to our concerns here. Although the patients did not recognize familiar faces presented in photographs, their skin conductance did react—and only to the faces of persons they knew, not to unfamiliar ones. The authors concluded from this that "an early step in the physiological process of recognition is still taking place but that the results of its operation are not being made available to consciousness." They suggest that discrimination among stimuli takes place only on an unconscious level.[11] This describes in physiological terms what I have been proposing above!

Similarly, the neurologist Oliver Sacks has shown how damage to the higher brain centers can "free" empathic connectedness on the level of the autonomic nervous system.[12] Receptive aphasia is a condition in which the patient is incapable of understanding the meaning of words although able to hear them. Yet it can be demonstrated that such patients are able to understand what is said to them if the signals usually accompanying spoken language are present: tone of voice, intonation, facial expression, gestures, body posture. These are communicated via the autonomic nervous system and its proprioceptive pathways, which transmit the deep sensibility of the muscles. This deep sensibility is also a part of our empathic perceptual processes.

Communication, therefore, does not take place through words alone; it is embedded in other forms of expression that transcend the purely verbal. Receptivity to these is especially pronounced in aphasic individuals. For them, as Sacks writes, "with emotionally laden utterance, the meaning may be fully grasped even when every word is missed.... [I sometimes have the feeling] which all of us who work closely with aphasics have—that one cannot lie to an aphasic. He cannot grasp your words, and so he cannot be deceived by them; but what he grasps with infallible precision [is] namely the *expression* that goes with the words, that total, spontaneous, involuntary expressiveness which can never be simulated or faked, as words alone can, all too easily."[13]

This makes it clear that language acquisition is not only a part of acculturation but that it also involves the adoption of stereotypical ways of thinking that adapt us to our society and distort our perceptions as well. Consequently, the "removal" of language through brain damage removes the inhibition of our early fundamental perceptual processes *and* of our empathic capacity that has been suppressed by our learning of language.

Oliver Sacks reports that he was once met by a roar of laughter on entering his aphasia ward. The patients were just beginning to watch a televised speech by President Reagan and were eager to continue watching it.[14]

There he was, the old charmer, the actor with the practiced rhetoric, his histrionics, his emotional appeal—and all the patients were convulsed with laughter.... The president is generally thought to be a moving speaker—but he was moving them, apparently, mainly to laughter.... "One can lie with the mouth," Nietzsche writes, "but with the accompanying grimace one nevertheless tells the truth." To such a grimace, to any falsity or impropriety in bodily appearance or posture, aphasiacs are preternaturally sensitive. And if they cannot see one—this is especially true of our blind aphasiacs— they have an infallible ear for every vocal nuance, the tone, the rhythm, the cadences, the music, the subtlest modulations, inflections, intonations, which can give, or remove, verisimilitude from a man's voice.

In this, then, lies their power of understanding— understanding, without words, what is authentic or inauthentic. Thus it was the grimaces, the histrionisms, the gestures— and, above all, the tones and cadences of the President's voice—that rang false for these wordless but immensely sensitive patients. It was to these (for them) most glaring, even grotesque, incongruities and improprieties that my aphasiac patients responded, undeceived and undeceivable by words.

This is why they laughed at the President's speech.[15]

The question that arises here is whether these patients would have had access to their deeper perceptions without their brain injuries. All people have the capacity for sensitivity, but they differ in the degree to which their sensitivity reaches a conscious level. Yet since language acquisition is part and parcel of the process that makes us lose contact with our sensitivity, many of us end up fooled by mere appearance. Thus, Sacks concludes his report: "And so cunningly was deceptive word use combined with deceptive tone, that it was the brain-damaged who remained undeceived."[16]

Some of us are so easily deceived because of our need to collaborate in the deception in order to maintain our own dissociation. In this connection, I should like to return to Alexander and Margarete Mitscherlich's study of Germans' inability to come to terms with grief. The authors attributed their lack of therapeutic success to their patients' loss of a narcissistic object choice. Since Hitler was the internalized object with whom they had identified, by losing him their egos were impoverished.[17]

This thesis demonstrates in exemplary fashion, I believe, how abstract (psychological) ideas obscure our vision of what is actually going on. If we proceed a priori from the concept of narcissism, we shall miss seeing that these patients suffered from a much more fundamental illness: their psychological development had been based on a kind of identification that prevented inner authenticity. Therefore, they could not mourn. Their self was impoverished even before they identified with Hitler, and it was *because of* this impoverishment that they identified with him. The emphasis on "object choice" misses the point that this choice serves a special purpose: namely, that of avoiding the self. The lost object (Hitler) was simply the means of keeping them from developing a self of their own. To mourn the actual loss (of their soul), on the other hand, would have meant daring to risk the collapse of a personality structure based on externals. Furthermore, in such cases a patient cannot be helped with a strictly theoretical model that fails to take cognizance of the true nature of the illness and of the fear both patient and therapist would have to face.

How can we face the murderousness of artificial feelings? Let us take the example of the SS men who carried out the destruction of Oradour and the murder of all its inhabitants in occupied France. This event raises the question of whether devotion to death makes it totally impossible for people to regain contact with their own feelings. Ernst von Schenck reports that the SS men carried out this gruesome deed with absolute calm. After all the men of the town had been shot, the women and children were taken to the church, which was then set afire. All those inside burned to death. The SS men had gathered together the women and children "with utmost kindness. The mothers were moved by so much tenderness on the part of these feared men, who hugged the children, carefully took them in their arms, joked with them, or like young fathers gently put them in their baby carriages, so that the poor doomed women followed as though they were on their way to a splendid celebration of reconciliation. When they were all inside the church, the doors were locked, and the mass murder could begin."[18]

This horrendous event testifies to the way feelings can be murdered in the name of feelings. Herein lies the similarity to Ronald Reagan's speech discussed above. The aphasic patients laughed because they were aware of the discrepancy between the feelings displayed for effect (friendliness, joviality, love) and the reality behind Reagan's grimaces: arrogance and hatred.

Ernst von Schenck writes of the SS men: "I am convinced that when these SS men were holding a French child in their arms, they were not weighed down by the slightest feeling of hatred. . . . And I am further convinced that if the order had suddenly been countermanded (how easily it might have been, for it was an error; another town was actually meant to be 'reprimanded'), they would have gone on playing the good daddy with conviction and might even have told the mothers about their original evil intentions as a kind of macabre joke. But orders are orders!"[19]

The coexistence of "decent" feelings and unacknowledged murderousness is a clear sign that all a person's feelings are not rooted in the inner self. If we try to explain such events by the exceptional nature of the circumstances, we shall miss their true significance and basic character. A case in point is the story of the American co-ed who shot herself rather than her dog. She had spent the night with a man, and her parents demanded she shoot her dog as "punishment." They wanted to teach their daughter a lesson—simply "for her own good."[20] Naturally, they were distraught by the result of their "loving" intentions. This could have happened only because they thought they were acting on the basis of their feelings; yet their alleged feelings of kindness were artificial, and the real emotions guiding their actions were murderous.

Sometimes we catch a direct glimpse of the self-hatred behind all this. It becomes patent in the glorification of death, which, as we have said, is especially common among the adherents of fascism. These people are only doing openly what in other cases is hidden behind the veneer of pleasantness: the pursuit of death keeps many people—not only fascists—alive.

On October 12, 1936, Franco's General Millán Astray cast his spell on the University of Salamanca with the paradoxical battle cry he had introduced among his troops: "Long live Death!" And, in the course of his inflammatory speech, he continued: "The Basque country and Catalonia are two cancers in the body of the nation. Fascism, Spain's salvation, knows how to remove them. Like a resolute surgeon it will cut into the living flesh without sentimentality. And since the healthy flesh is the soil and the diseased flesh the people living on it, fascism and the army will eradicate the people and restore the soil as the nation's sacred possession."[21]

Such people make it quite obvious that they pursue destruction to find relief from inner emptiness. We can see clearly what was not so apparent in the case of Wilhelm Kütemeyer's patient who never felt so well as when he was in danger. His inner malaise became intolerable when the war was over and he was no longer able to engage in destructive activities. He then began to take morphine, for in this way, as he reported to Kütemeyer, "the coldness I feel inside thaws, [and] this horrible cramp under my heart dissolves."[22]

There exists, then, a breed of men whose central and continuing preoccupation is death. We know that Hitler and his henchmen instigated and committed murder, but we fail to recognize that they are representative of the type of person to whom only death and destruction give a sense of aliveness. In his prison diaries, Albert Speer describes Hitler's love of the destructive force of fire:

That he set the world aflame and brought fire and sword upon the Continent—such statements may be mere imagery. But fire itself, literally and directly, always stirred a profound excitement in him. I recall his ordering showings in the Chancellery of the films of burning London, of the sea of flames over Warsaw, of exploding convoys, and the rapture with which he watched those films. I never saw him so worked up as toward the end of the war, when in a kind of delirium he pictured for himself and for us the destruction of New York in a hurricane of fire. He described the skyscrapers being turned into gigantic burning torches, collapsing upon one another, the glow of the exploding city illuminating the dark sky.[23]

Ernst Jünger, a novelist and German army officer in both world wars, made the following comment about Hitler in his diaries in October 1944: "The frenetic acclamation accompanying his appearance was actually the assent to self-destruction."[24]

In her autobiographical account, *Den Wolf umarmen* ("Embracing the Wolf"), Luise Rinser describes the experience of a fatherly friend who protected her from National Socialism in the early days of the Third Reich when she was a young teacher: "[Dr. Stein] had gone to Hitler's residence on the Obersalzberg one day to see Hitler face-to-face. He was standing in the third row among those waiting for the Führer in the garden. *He* appeared, patted the children on the head, greeted one person and the other, and, hand raised in the air in a perverse blessing, moved on. *He* had already passed the place where Dr. Stein was standing, but after going several yards, *he* suddenly turned, stopped short, and then went directly up to him, gave him his hand across the two front rows, and looked him straight in the eye as if imploringly. Dr. Stein was thrown into confusion. At that very moment he had had the clear and distinct thought that the murder of tyrants should be permissible."[25]

Clearly, Hitler felt attracted to death and destruction in whatever form. That he could sense the presence—although not the target—of murderous thoughts in someone standing

at a distance from him shows how intense was his preoccupation. I am not speaking here of any supernatural gifts,
but simply pointing out the fact that such people can perceive
any correspondence to their own murderous propensities.

The commitment to destruction and death is by no means
diminished by "abreaction," although it is a widespread
view that anger and rage can be diminished if just given a
chance to be expressed. But catharsis does not work for those
people whose anger and rage are fueled by self-hatred, for if
it is projected onto an external object, self-hatred is only
intensified and is aggravated by actions that are unconsciously perceived deep within as further forms of self-
betrayal. Thus, with every additional act of destruction,
destructive rage raises its stakes.

We can actually see this happening every day. The only
thing that can halt such people's ever-increasing lust for
destruction is sheer physical exhaustion. All conquerors—
whether in the field of politics or of industry—are unable to
stop once embarked on this road. The less able they are to
devote themselves to the conquest of their inner world, the
more obstinately they storm ahead on the escape route from
themselves and intensify their search for conquest beyond
the confines of the hated self.

When their power plays fail, they begin to "suffer." But
their kind of suffering is completely different from the kind
that comes from despair at not finding a loving link to humanity. People who attempt to remain in contact with their
inner world are trying to overcome isolation and to experience love and warmth. Individuals who have forsaken their
inner reality for power, however, have ceased being sustained by the hope of this link to humanity. They suffer
because their power plays have failed. And this failure
threatens them with the chaos of a dissociated self, which
they will try to escape by desperately redoubling their efforts
to remain in control and by placing the blame for their own
failure on others. Self-pity, not sorrow, will mark their "suffering."

Whatever "feelings" they show are displayed merely for effect. Even committing suicide is only part of a drama they are performing. To take one's life because one can no longer stand oneself as a result of one's deeds would at least be a sign of shame and the admission of a terrible self-distortion. But this was not the case with Hitler, who told Albert Speer: "Believe me, Speer, it is easy for me to end my life. A brief moment and I'm freed of everything, liberated from this painful existence."[26] Only an empty and meaningless life is ended so easily. That he turned life into hell for other people did not even enter Hitler's consciousness; he experienced only self-pity. A basic contempt for life is transformed into a denial of life and, at the same time, a glorification of death.

We must differentiate here between two different forms of suffering that typify two completely different kinds of human development—otherwise our compassion will play a trick on us. For if we are not aware that a given individual is suffering out of self-pity for failed power plays, our compassion will merely reinforce that person's contempt for us instead of leading to healing him or her. Such people are the best candidates for pharmacological therapy, since with drugs we can very successfully suppress their inner tensions while maintaining their dissociated state. These "cures," however, "become weapons against fundamental involvement, instead of acting as its facilitators," as Martti Siirala so correctly puts it.[27] With pharmacological therapies, we only help patients to avoid dealing with life. The failure of this type of therapy is obscured by talk of restoring patients to their previous levels of "effectiveness."

The nature of self-hatred is so well hidden from us because we all let ourselves be too easily impressed by power. We always attribute strength to those with power and thus assume that they know more about life and are better human beings than we, who are, after all, only "failures." In fact, genuine strength lies in the ability to tolerate psychic pain; as a rule, however, we think those people are strong who know no fear, especially no fear of death. Yet those who glorify and are devoted to death are not "overcoming" it—they are merely denying their fear of it. These are the people who have not been able to bear the pain caused by their parents' inadequate love and have therefore invented the myth that sensitivity to inner pain denotes weakness.

And thus it is: people who have dissociated what for them was unbearable pain and suffering are the champions and guardians of a distorted picture of reality. Because they could not tolerate their own weakness in the face of a manipulative pseudolove, they spend a lifetime acquiring power and possessions. This saves them from having to confront the self-hatred caused by having submitted to a false love. And their "delusional possession of reality," as Martti Siirala has called it, has become what necessarily defines masculine strength. We find, consequently, "strong men" cut off from their deepest feelings because they do not have the strength to bear them. This total inversion of psychic reality is so difficult to see through because these same "strong men," whose life business it is to be in power, by virtue of their dominant position in society, articulate and determine our definition of reality.

Feelings That Are Not Feelings

ALTHOUGH I HAVE referred repeatedly in previous chapters to pseudofeelings, I would like to subject them to scrutiny here. We all desperately want the appearance of things to correspond to the truth, for this helps to assuage our doubts about the reliability of our empathic perceptions. Consequently, we are shocked when we discover that truth and appearance are not identical. This is especially the case when we are confronted with the eruption of violence on the part of people whose perfect social image has made us think they were models of "real" feelings. In contrast, we are not dismayed or even surprised when violence is employed in the defense of law and order. I would like to examine this contradiction in the present chapter by analyzing several specific cases.

The Sudden Killer

On a winter evening in 1975, Gregg Sanders murdered his mother and father with an ax.[1]

Gregg was fifteen years old at the time and was regarded as a model student at the exclusive private school he was attending. He had been no problem whatsoever, and there had been no discernible warning signs, according to the assistant headmaster of the school. His neighbors described him as a thoughtful and courteous boy. On the afternoon of the murders, according to his teachers, he showed no signs of tension or anxiety. On the same day, an English paper he had written was read aloud in class as an example of excellent work. It described an imaginary conversation between Jesus and God and was titled "Father Knows Best." In it, between the Crucifixion and the Resurrection a stern God orders Jesus to return to earth and await his Father's call.

Gregg's father was vice-president of a major New York bank, and his mother, a teacher, worked at a church day-care center. Both placed all their ambition in their son and constantly pressured him to achieve, although he was already an honor student. A friend said about him, "To hear him talk you'd think he was on the borderline of failing." During Gregg's first year at the private school, his adviser took notes on a conference with the parents: "they still feel Gregg does not do too much work at home. He seems to be able to get good grades without exerting himself, but I know they feel that even better grades might be possible with more effort at home."

The family pediatrician described the mother as a rigid and withdrawn woman. When she was once asked whether she wanted to discuss any problems Gregg might have, she replied abruptly, "We have no problems." Yet three years before the murders, Gregg suffered from dizzy spells over an eight-month period, which his mother attributed to purely organic sources. The electroencephalogram she requested showed normal brain function.

When Gregg's adviser at school invited the mother to come in for a routine conference—Gregg himself had never spoken of problems—she said that was unnecessary since she was satisfied with her son's grades and the school. This was three months prior to the murders. The mother was also described as a socially conscious woman who worked at the church day-care center only because she thought it wrong to let her training as a teacher go to waste. Her friends remembered her stoicism in going to work every day although she suffered from chronic back pain and a neck injury sustained in an automobile accident. And they also told of "her devotion to Gregg and his apparent love and concern for her."

The father was described as a man who had worked hard to achieve the American dream. He had begun as the son of a longshoreman in Philadelphia and rose to be vice-president of a large bank. He often brought his work home with him, and Gregg would sometimes tell his friends how hard his father worked and what a responsible job he had.

What emerges here is a picture of parents driven by the concepts of duty and success, who denied all feelings that would point in other directions. Thus, the mother even denied her physical pain because she must practice her profession as teacher. About her son's future she once wrote, "We hope that Gregg will want to go to college, but that whatever he does, he does happily and well." She used the word "happily," however, without any regard for the freedom happiness presupposes. For this poor woman, happiness meant nothing more than the absence of a brain defect in her boy.

It is more than clear that these parents who were so preoccupied with success knew nothing about their son's inner life. Friends and neighbors, too, had no inkling of it. Yet there were sufficient signs of an inner split:

• He told a friend about an episode he had experienced when he was five. Once when his father barged into his room, it made the boy so furious that he did not speak to him for three weeks. Already, he experienced his father as an intruder.

• His sister reported how on occasion he would "rail and curse" at their father and hit the wall in rage. Later, he would have no memory of these outbursts. Clearly, these were indications of a dissociation between rage and submission to the norms of proper behavior and an outer-directed identity. On the inside destructiveness and outside the shell of conformity to parental wishes—this tension caused a split in the "wholeness" of his personality.

• A split was further evidenced by a strange interest that was not revealed until later: He had a secret room, a ten-foot-long crawl space he entered through a hidden opening in his bedroom. There he kept a mattress, a lamp, books, empty liquor bottles, and a large swastika on a wooden panel, along with other Nazi emblems as well as a six-page handwritten manuscript filled with quotations from Adolf Hitler.

No one was aware of this interest of his. In political discussions he took liberal positions and told in school of how he had argued with his father, who was a supporter of President Nixon. Once when asked by a teacher during a class discussion what he thought of Hitler, he replied, "He was a genius; unfortunately he was insane." And he did not like Himmler because he was a sadist.

There were other signs of his inner conflict:

• He told a friend exactly how he intended to kill himself. He would go to the unused water tower outside of town, go up its exterior stairs, and climb over the fence at the top. He would hang over the edge by one hand and then slash his wrist. He emphasized that he would not slash his wrist first because that might prevent him from climbing the fence. This was exactly how Gregg committed suicide after killing his parents!

• He told the same friend that he thought shooting someone was an impersonal way to kill. A strange remark, but one that reflects the intensity of his murderous desires. On the other hand, his later suicide note avoided completely any tone of personal involvement; in it, he wanted to appear considerate and proper. This was in keeping with his past behavior.

• When he was eleven, he had a discussion with a friend about a man in a neighboring town who had murdered his wife, mother, and three children. The man wrote a letter explaining that he had shot his family to spare them sorrow and to save their souls. Whereas Gregg's friend was frightened by the case, Gregg asserted that he was not. He had even kept a file of news stories about the murder.

What precipitated the murder of his parents and his subsequent suicide? Four days before he killed them, he had been reprimanded by his history teacher; something like this had never happened to him before. The teacher threatened him with a demerit for talking in class. Ordinarily, this meant that a letter was sent home to the parents. The next day Gregg told his best friend that he now had three options: "I can beat up the teacher, I can intercept the letter, or I can kill myself." We see here how little resilience is possessed by a self totally organized according to parental wishes when its image that has been taken for genuine is threatened with deflation. As a matter of fact, nothing happened to the boy; the teacher had not carried out his threat, and neither the headmaster nor the parents learned anything about Gregg's infraction. But in this family everything was centered on image. When his older sister dropped out of college, his parents were not interested in her problems; they were concerned only about the effect her decision to leave school would have on their social standing.

Toward the end of the school day on which Gregg would murder his parents he discussed with fellow students the courses they would take the following year. No one noticed anything unusual about him. At home he ate dinner with his parents. Then—the state medical examiner said that it was at approximately 9:30 P.M.—Gregg took a two-foot ax and killed his father with several blows to the head while he was sitting in the kitchen working on bank reports. His mother, already in her nightclothes, was murdered in the dining room. He then walked to the water tower, climbed to the top, slashed his wrist, and jumped.

Even in the act of murder, he clung fast to the image he had of himself. He left the following note on his desk: "To whom it may concern: I am sorry for the trouble I have caused. I'm not in any way mad at my parents. I just can't take it anymore. Well, I just wanted to say I'm sorry. Good luck. Gregg Sanders."

Those who have totally committed themselves to image and appearance will take the "feelings" Gregg expressed here as evidence of remorse and concern. His sister, in a letter written to the local police department, "concluded that Gregg had killed his parents out of love for them, to spare them the sorrow of living with his suicide." And many, in order to suppress their own inner stirrings of hatred, will accept the way she turns his hatred into love. She writes: "For reasons that will never be known to me or anyone, my brother could not cope with the pressures of his life anymore. What pressures can a 15-year-old have? . . . Gregg was an extremely sensitive and loving boy, so perhaps the usual pressures hit him harder than most children his age."

The real issue here: the love that must be earned produces a type of self-esteem based solely on the fulfillment of demands for performance. Hatred is the result. Only those who are able to acknowledge their own injuries will recognize the real sources of Gregg's terrible deed. To perceive the hatred that drove and destroyed the boy, we need to recognize how it gnaws at us too.

Apparently, Gregg's inner disintegration was hastened by his desperate attempt to live up to the myths with which he grew up. Those, on the other hand, who live by these myths without feeling that image and actions must correspond to each other have successfully adapted to the pervasive hypocrisy of our culture and know how to "sublimate" their destructiveness in socially acceptable ways. The tragedy of people like Gregg is that they cannot be hypocritical. When their murderousness breaks through, they actually kill the source of their malaise. The "truly" well-adjusted, who have learned to be hypocritical, murder instead—in an entirely legal manner—those who remind them of their own self-betrayal.

Killers with a Good Conscience

Before I turn to a consideration of officially sanctioned murder, I would like to say a few words about so-called sublimation. The psychoanalytic concept of sublimation is based on the notion that human beings are governed by primitive instincts whose energy must be diverted into socially "more acceptable" channels. Freud said that "instincts can change their aim (by displacement)."[2] In his view, the two "basic instincts" of eros and destructiveness could be either repressed or sublimated. To the present day, this approach has hindered an investigation of how destructiveness and aggressiveness actually develop.[3] By declaring sublimation to be the only way to counter human destructiveness, Freud lent support to those ideologies that see human beings as innately destructive and implicitly glorify this condition as our "natural" state.

Yet we can escape the dead end of the drive theory if we acknowledge that sublimation does not even begin to affect the real sources of destructiveness and aggression; it merely directs them into channels acceptable at the moment—for example, into the business world with its cutthroat competition. The only way to deal with destructiveness is to face the helplessness that brought it about in the first place.

It is only by accepting our helplessness and recognizing the limits it sets that we can be liberated from a mythical sense of guilt for being small and insignificant. Only by giving up the idea that helplessness is a sign of failure can we free ourselves from primitive and destructive rage. Both repression and sublimation, on the other hand, keep the sources of this rage alive.

In addition, the theory of sublimation encourages a kind of reformist thinking that downplays the reality of violence by tolerating it and according it a false understanding. If all we do is divert violent impulses toward less harmful outlets, then we need not confront the crucial question of whether we control our demons or they control us.

A telling example of how widespread the view is that our demons control us is afforded by the events surrounding the Attica prison revolt on September 9, 1971. On that day, nearly thirteen hundred prisoners, approximately half of Attica's inmates, captured more than three dozen guards and civilian employees of the prison and held them hostage for four tense days of negotiations. On orders of the governor of New York, Nelson A. Rockefeller, the state police retook the prison by force on September 13.

The background and events of the revolt have been exhaustively documented.[4] Attica prison was extremely overcrowded; the inmates were mainly black and Puerto Rican. Militancy and demands for prisoners' rights were on the rise. The revolt began with an incident on the afternoon of September 8: a corrections officer, thinking that two inmates were fighting, came up behind them and placed his hand on one of them. The latter spun around and hit the guard, apparently quite instinctively, not having seen who was behind him. The two prisoners, one black and one white, had merely been practicing for the prison football team—the white man was doing the coaching—when the prison guard, mistaking their behavior for fighting, intervened.

After the inmates had been locked in their cells for the night, the two involved in the incident were taken from their cells and put into solitary confinement. Soon a rumor spread that they had been beaten. By the next morning, the rebellion was under way. The prisoners demanded minimal reforms and amnesty for the protesters.

Governor Rockefeller ordered the use of force to restore order after steadfastly refusing to take part in negotiations for a peaceful settlement, even though these were already being conducted by a citizens' committee under the leadership of the commissioner of the state's Department of Corrections. Immediately after the revolt had been quelled, Rockefeller announced that the state police and prison personnel had done a "superb job." The result of this "superb job" was that twenty-nine inmates and ten hostages had been killed and eighty-nine others wounded. Official investigations attributed this bloodbath to indiscriminate and unwarranted gunfire on the part of the attacking force.

Setting aside the governor's political responsibility, I am concerned here solely with the actions of the men who stormed the prison. They were ostensibly charged with freeing the hostages, and their orders were to avoid shooting unless in self-defense or in defense of others.

The prisoners had in their possession two tear-gas guns, as well as clubs and knives. The assault force, one thousand strong, was armed with shotguns, pistols, and rifles. At a distance of fifty yards, buckshot from the shotguns could hit anywhere within an area four feet in diameter; obviously, they were not designed to deal with a threat from specific individuals. In the crowded prison yard, the pellets were bound to strike people at random. One stray pellet, for example, fatally wounded one of the hostages.

During the riot, the hostages were guarded by Black Muslims, clearly recognizable by their shaved heads. After the ultimatum to surrender was delivered to the prisoners, the Black Muslims forced eight hostages to lie on the floor and held knives to their throats. This act signaled that the ultimatum had been rejected, and the police then stormed the prison. They had orders not to shoot as long as nothing happened to the hostages. Prior to the police attack, a rumor circulated that hostages had been castrated. This form of bestiality corresponded so exactly to expectation that the police and prison guards at first attributed the death of the ten hostages to the alleged mutilation by the prisoners. By the second day following the attack, however, it was established that all the deaths had been caused solely by police bullets.

How are we to view men who storm a prison with

shotguns—weapons that kill and maim indiscriminately—although they know the inmates who are their potential targets surround the hostages they want to free? How did their choice of weapon fit their purpose?

Tom Wicker of the *New York Times* wrote three days later: "Even the strong belief that an assault on the stronghold would cause prisoners to kill the 38 hostages seemed to make little difference to those who had the guns; they wanted to go in." That was exactly it: they *wanted* to go in and kill! They were in a fury totally unrelated to their mission of freeing the hostages and putting down the revolt of an essentially unarmed group of prisoners. They were obsessed by the rumor of castration; it spurred them on, and it was nothing other than an expression of their own destructiveness projected onto people they considered inferior and worthless.

We must keep in mind that a criminal in prison faces people who are very poorly paid, have scarcely any education, and stand on the lowest rungs of the social ladder. Yet they are clothed with authority, a boon to someone suffering from low self-esteem due to low social status. In this way, society puts itself into a contradictory position: on the one hand, it seeks to punish those who break the law but, on the other, is unwilling to pay the price of running a prison system that might do something to rehabilitate those entrusted to its care. Therefore, society itself is ultimately responsible for the Attica tragedy.

Further, what happened at Attica throws light on those who, although themselves victims of social inequity, identify all the more with authoritarian structures. At Attica, the state police, as well as the prison guards, were—like the prisoners—subject to an unbending discipline and routine. Even though they were in the position of ordering other human beings around, they were nonetheless themselves prisoners in a prison. But the frustrations of their job naturally had one outlet: the criminal declared by law to be inferior to them. For those who are prepared to obey because obedience has come to give meaning to their lives, the person officially declared weak becomes the scapegoat, the object of their pent-up rage. In this case, the "weak" one is the criminal, the rebel, the outsider, who has the effrontery to demand to be treated humanely.

The events at Attica show in concrete fashion how a lack of autonomy can produce rage and destructiveness on such a scale that the resulting actions are out of all proportion to the occasion. We see here in raw form what is ordinarily hidden from view: the dependency generated by obedience takes its revenge under the cloak of socially acceptable behavior. The attackers feel justified in killing prisoners considered less than human. For their actions they then expect praise. And the governor was lavish with this, thereby legitimizing out-and-out murder.

Official blessings lay the groundwork for more and more violence, since the guilt necessarily caused by such actions must be warded off unceasingly by increased brutality. The terrible story of Attica is the story of what obedience and conformity do to human beings.

Not only criminals tend toward violence; it is present in all of us who live in a world in which the fundamental motive for action is a willingness to obey. If we can love ourselves only because we are obedient, we will feel righteous when we kill in others the impulse to disobedience that once was our own. We need enemies not only to protect us from the old enemy within but also as a way of discharging our growing pent-up rage.

And while actually hating and despising life, we think ourselves kind, generous, and concerned about others. Yet the truth of the matter is that we are trying to appear "proper," in other words, to fulfill others' expectations, for only then can we love ourselves. *That* is true narcissism, and it is fostered very effectively by our culture. We love a "proper" facade, not the self we could be.

Depersonalized Violence

Conforming to social norms can very easily lead to indulging in violent tendencies while at the same time denying it. On March 27, 1979, during a political demonstration in Switzerland, a writer was arrested by two policemen who beat him with clubs. One of the policemen, when later cross-examined by a judge, stated: "What do you expect of me? I have always had to obey somebody: as a child, as a school-boy, as an apprentice, as a soldier, and now as a policeman. So I simply carried out the orders."[5]

Of course, he had been instructed to preserve order. Using this excuse, the policemen simply beat a man. What is inter-esting here is not so much the fact that in court one of them said in his defense that he was acting on orders but that he summed up the evolution of obedience per se: we are brought up to obey but not to think or feel for ourselves. What remains obscured is that our training is the very source of what society fears and thereby seeks in vain to defend itself against—namely, destructiveness.

The destructiveness in these examples has two aspects. It leads, on the one hand, to continually renewed suppression of one's potential for aliveness; on the other, to overt vio-lence against anyone identified as socially "deviant" or of-fensive. And the bureaucratization of life works in yet another way. It not only permits the use of violence not acknowledged as such, but it also destroys people by causing them to distance themselves from their feelings, which is also exactly what happens as a result of accepting the duty to be obedient.

In this connection, I would like to quote Henry T. Nash, a former intelligence analyst for the Pentagon:

> As an analyst in the Political and Economics Section of the Air Targets Division my responsibility was to "nominate" as tar-gets buildings identified as Communist Party headquarters located in various Soviet cities. . . . While I worked at selecting

and justifying political targets, fellow analysts in other offices were busy identifying different types of strategic targets—petroleum depots, airfields, or industrial centers. Each of us made nominations ... and we each hoped that our targets would be chosen for a DOD strategic plan of nuclear attack designed to bring about a rapid, unconditional surrender of Soviet forces. Like myself, my colleagues were graduates of liberal arts colleges and many were taking evening graduate courses in fields such as international relations or economic theory.... Today ... I am frequently visited by haunting memories of my work.... [W]hat was it about work with Air Targets that made me insensitive to its homicidal implications? ... [We] drank coffee and ate lunch, never experienced guilt or self-criticism.... What enabled us calmly to plan to incinerate vast numbers of unknown human beings without any sense of moral revulsion? At least no signs of moral revulsion surfaced when we were having an extra martini or two at lunch to celebrate the inclusion of some of our government control centers in a Joint Chiefs list of prime Soviet targets.[6]

The author notes many of the features that made this kind of work possible. The Cold War made his job of selecting targets in the Soviet Union seem respectable. Since the analysts always worked only on details and were not familiar with the total picture, their consciences remained clear. Always anticipating the worst from the enemy allowed them to project their own fantasies freely without having to measure them against reality. Nash goes on, "Immunity from criticism was assured by the fact that each analyst's conclusions, or those of his team, would be immediately classified [as secret]." In addition, the hierarchical structure of the bureaucracy itself served to divert attention from the destructive nature of the work. What people really thought about was where they stood in relation to others. Another way of obscuring the reality of what their work was about was the neutralization of the language used. "Civil servants felt more comfortable with Defense Department than War Department; targets for attack as in the

Vietnam War were given the name 'strategic hamlet,' bombing raids became 'surgical strikes,' the enemy was not killed but 'taken out,' a military ground offensive was termed 'aggressive defense.' "[7]

Nash tells of being back in Washington and talking with old friends and co-workers: "It's all very much as I remember it—people whose speech and behavior suggest their sociability, but also their strong conviction that they are doing what needs to be done and it is therefore right. Nothing in the air seems sinister or hints of guilt. There is still the working atmosphere of a bank or insurance company."[8] The point here is that obedience necessitates suppressing those feelings that could counteract this behavior. If we must kill the potential for empathy in ourselves, we will not have genuine feelings anymore. All that will be left is the focus on achievement, which will bring us the recognition on which our self-esteem depends. Any criticism will be met with indignant self-pity.

It is the security a bureaucratic life offers in a world experienced as chaotic that makes it so attractive. George W. S. Trow highlighted this aspect in his analysis of "the *new, tough reality* in American life," describing the fate of a tract of land, Black Rock Forest, given to Harvard University.[9] Even though politicians often make a point of differentiating between the mentality of bureaucrats and members of corporate structures, common to both is stereotypical thinking. The successful manager and the successful civil servant are skillful in manipulating stereotypes. Both take advantage of people's reluctance to try something new, which would add to the threat of chaos and thus to their inner dread.

Black Rock Forest was donated to Harvard in 1949 for purposes of conservation research. But after the Second World War, according to Trow, the university began "looking closely, ruthlessly at its assets. . . . [T]he work of running the university was separated from the work of maintaining its particular character."[10] This came about in the same way that individuals cut themselves off from the inner life. Here, self-betrayal was in a sense given official sanction. The reality of the business world—that an asset is suspect if it does not produce a profit—became the operating dogma of the university. Whereas Harvard had been renowned in the past for pursuing humanistic goals opposed to those of business, it now changed its course: "There is no distance now between Harvard and the outside world; you could not find the boundary. The context of Harvard is the same as the context of the *Times*, which is the large context of the whole country. . . ."[11]

Trow notes that Black Rock Forest was by no means a financial burden, for the income from the endowment intended for its maintenance had actually increased. But modern bookkeeping had difficulty dealing with this. Therefore, the new managers of Harvard decided to get rid of this thorn in their side, having adopted the new market value method of accounting on July 1, 1970. The true value of the forest lay in its beauty, its abundance of life, and the importance of the conservation work being done there. Yet for the New Man in the accounting department, these things no longer mattered. Trow describes him this way: "He was represented as having a point of view, but what he had in fact was a function and a tone of voice. . . . His tone of voice was neutral. This neutral tone of voice was his point of view. He was never asked to explain himself; his voice explained him."[12]

This is an exemplary case of image replacing feelings. The resulting impersonality is the new force that increasingly rules the world. These clever people, whose capacity for "adjustment" has made them what they are, ally themselves with this impersonality, for that enables them to escape responsibility. People who have a connection to their inner world, the "idealists," struggle against this trend, but their struggle is a difficult one, since the new norms are defended with artificial feelings ("progress" and "security" are supposedly in danger). The real feelings, fueled by fear of chaos and hidden behind the mask of impersonality and the image of resoluteness ("point of view"), are destructive. Those in our society who are most successful in presenting an image of self-confidence will fool those who are desperately seeking self-confidence themselves and are grateful to find someone who *appears* to be self-confident.

The university decided to sell the forest, whose beauty and integrity were thus lost to everyone, and only because an "up-to-date" accounting method was incapable of considering anything that didn't produce an obvious profit.

Violence in Defense of the Basic Lie

At the same time that obedience distances people from their inner lives, it also protects them from anxiety generated by their loss of autonomy. There are many varieties of obedient behavior. Common to all is the need to maintain the lie about love. Submission to this lie is equated with "living in the real world." But those who have retained the ability to integrate inner and outer worlds will find this kind of reality insane.

When Andrei Sakharov, the Soviet human rights advocate and Nobel Peace Prize winner, was exiled to Gorky, a campaign of defamation was organized against him and his wife, Elena Bonner. It took especially vicious form against her; the Sakharovs were even afraid to go to the bakery for fear of insults such as, "Your Yid wife must be killed." Elena Bonner, an excellent pediatrician, had cured a neighbor's child whose allergies had been unsuccessfully treated by physicians in Gorky. After the smear campaign got under way, the child's mother cried, "It would have been better for my child to rot than to be touched by your dirty hands."[13] This mother submitted so completely to official views that she not only became furious at Elena Bonner's helpfulness but also expressed hatred for her own child.

"We are a great united community," reads a sentence in

a 1941 Nazi propaganda tract by the "Arbeitsmaiden," an association of young women who performed compulsory work. Now, over forty years later, its former leaders still repeat the same sentiments, and this in spite of the subsequently documented sadistic way the members under their command were treated at the time. It is not that these women are lying in the usual sense of the word but that, as Countess Sybil Schönfeldt correctly analyzes, they cannot face the fact that they had so cheerfully submitted to a violent dictatorship.[14] The lie is that they were motivated by love; they are denying the subliminal hatred involved. The responsibility of the female work corps, according to the official definition, was "education for National Socialism." And here are Hitler's words on the subject of the education of youth in the Third Reich: "A young generation will grow up before which the world will tremble. I want the young to be violent, domineering, undismayed, cruel. . . . I don't want an intellectual type of education. Knowledge will only ruin my young people. . . . But they must learn self-control. They must learn to conquer their fear of death under the most difficult conditions."[15] The amazing thing here is that Hitler was quite open about his intentions, but these women still deny today that they relinquished the creativity of their own maternal nature for the sake of the male mythology of power.

The call for capital punishment clearly belongs in the context of our fear of inner chaos and our contempt for life, which upholds the Basic Lie. The advocates of capital punishment present their case with manifest feelings of outrage and insist that such punishment acts as a deterrent. A brief of the American Psychological Association submitted to the U.S. Supreme Court in December 1985 makes it clear that these "moral" feelings and arguments are an expression of murderous desires on the part of those who have surrendered their self to authority. The Court was considering the appeal of a prisoner who claimed that he had been denied a fair trial because the jury that convicted him of murder consisted solely of supporters of the death penalty. (This had to do with the stipulation in some states that no one opposed to the death penalty will be selected for jury duty in a murder trial.)[16]

The brief submitted by the psychologists summarized research showing that juries consisting only of supporters of the death penalty tend to go along with the prosecution's recommendations for sentencing, that they are not representative of the total population, and that approval of capital punishment prejudices the exercise of their function. In addition, they referred to various sociological studies showing that juries made up of supporters of the death penalty are more likely to find defendants guilty of more serious crimes than jurors who are against the death penalty. In cases that are not clear-cut, the brief states, jurors in favor of the death penalty are more likely to bring a guilty verdict than those opposed to it. Thus, in states where capital punishment is legal, jurors are selected according to whether or not they believe in it.[17]

What interests me here is not the questionable legal validity of such juries but the question of what kind of people are in favor of capital punishment. They are not representative of society as a whole, yet they presume to mete out justice in society's name. These are people who need to condemn someone, even to death. The emotional attitude they display on the surface, however, is a love of justice.

THE TRAGEDY OF My Lai during the Vietnam War is a famous and horrifying example of how killing compensates for feelings of insecurity about one's life. On March 16, 1968, more than four hundred people—men, women, and children—were herded together by a U.S. Army company and shot to death in the village of Son My in Quang Ngai province. It was a company that had just lost six soldiers in its first encounter with the Viet Cong; twelve men were also severely wounded by mines, which, it later turned out, had been planted by their own allies.[18]

This was a war being fought by soldiers under the banner of democratic values against an enemy they virtually never saw but on whom they wanted to take revenge for their losses. And thus My Lai, as Robert Jay Lifton puts it, afforded the American soldiers the momentary illusion "that in gunning down at point-blank range babies, women and old men, they were finally involved in a genuine military action—their elusive adversaries had finally been located, made to stand still, and annihilated—an illusion, in other words, that they had finally put their chaotic world back in order."[19]

A gigantic web of deadly deceit was fabricated surrounding United States involvement in this war. American soldiers were completely at a loss about their mission, but many were unable to confront this truth about themselves. The outer chaos, merely a reflection of the inner, could be put in order only by killing an external enemy. But there were a few like Ronald Ridenhour, who courageously exposed the truth about My Lai. Those, on the other hand, who hate themselves, mislead the rest of us with their platitudes about patriotism, bravery, and moral superiority. For the real feelings at work here are actually destructiveness and the compulsive need for an external enemy. From this we can conclude that "feelings" arising from a longing for order are never what they seem to be. They are an escape from one's inner chaos and necessarily result in destruction.

Our destructive intentions are often camouflaged. One manifestation of this is the perversion of empathy: instead of empathizing with the victim, we begin to pity the aggressor. There are numerous examples of this.

Although public opinion in the United States always clamors for law and order, it often sides with the killer in a murder case. In William Wright's book on the Claus von Bülow case, he writes that von Bülow, weary of his wealthy, stay-at-home wife, twice injected her with near-lethal doses of insulin, whereupon she lapsed into an irreversible coma. He was tried for attempted murder and found guilty.[20]

Within a short time, Claus von Bülow became a hero. His

supporters saw him as an underdog, the victim of a conspiracy to deprive him of an inheritance. They demonstrated outside the courthouse, wearing "Free Claus" T-shirts. He was asked in a television interview whether he had really intended to kill his wife, and when he, of course, denied this, the interviewer was visibly relieved. He was sentenced to ten years imprisonment on one count and twenty years on another but was released on one million dollars bail, having appealed the verdict. He went home to his Fifth Avenue apartment to await the outcome of his appeal. In the meantime, he gave fabulous parties and became the most sought-after man on the Manhattan dinner-party circuit.[21]

Similarly, there was a flood of public support for Richard Herrin, a Yale graduate student who smashed his girlfriend's skull with a hammer. He then went to the police and confessed. He told them that she went to sleep after the couple had spent an enjoyable evening together. He had planned the murder very carefully and methodically, and afterward he was not in the least out of control or unreasonable. Various groups from the Yale community immediately rallied to his defense: clergy and other members of the university's Catholic Center, faculty members, members of the administration, along with undergraduate and graduate students.[22]

The confessed murderer soon was released on bail and returned to classes temporarily. A well-known criminal lawyer took his case, and the jury found that the defendant, despite having committed an especially gruesome murder, was not guilty of murder but only of manslaughter in the first degree. The victim's parents were outraged, as were many others. Yet the Catholic clergy who had mobilized Herrin's defense spoke of "the message of forgiveness," and one of them, a nun, said she felt that everyone was capable of murder and she was grateful that *she* had not yet been led into temptation; she was convinced that it was only a matter of luck if one's murderous impulses were not triggered.[23] Her feelings of compassion for the murderer present a stark contrast to her astonishing calmness in the face of Herrin's heinous act.

Willard Gaylin, in his book analyzing the case, has every right to wonder why there was no revulsion over the murder of an innocent girl on the part of the clergy he interviewed. It is obvious that "compassion" for the murderer was a pretext used to ward off compassion for the victim, whose death was so cruel and untimely. That there was something else behind these manifested feelings is shown by the "amusement" expressed by the Catholic nun at Herrin's joke about his choice of a Harvard lawyer: "I guess people think it's so terrible that he could have made a joke two weeks after killing a girl. My response to that was 'He's alive enough to say to another Yalie, I chose a Harvard man.' "[24] This distorted reaction to the murderer's alleged "aliveness" not only prevents empathy for the victim from surfacing but effectively destroys it. The full extent to which genuine feelings were perverted is shown by the fact that no one from either the university or the Church went to the murdered girl's parents to express sympathy.

The above examples are not isolated phenomena. Something similar happens whenever empathy becomes a threat. An instructive commentary on this is afforded by two reports of German atrocities, one of barbarous German actions in occupied Belgium during the First World War, the other concerning the Holocaust during the Second World War. Atrocity stories about "the Huns" supposedly murdering women and children were actually part of the official propaganda effort to draw the United States into the First World War. The intent was to arouse hatred toward the Germans, and it succeeded. On the other hand, over twenty years later, when Americans began to hear about Hitler's "Final Solution," they reacted by and large with doubt and disbelief.

The lies about atrocities in the First World War were believed, whereas the true reports about the actual existence of "corpse factories" were not. Apart from the fact that leading public figures in the United States manipulated public opinion in connection with the Holocaust,[25] this situation also demonstrates very clearly that we tend to believe lies when they fuel our hatred, but it is difficult to believe those who would arouse our empathy.

Sometimes we hate the victims. They make us feel very uncomfortable; we are ashamed of our empathy because we hate the victim in ourselves. Our hatred stems from our shame for having allowed ourselves to become victims by surrendering our autonomy, and we want to avoid reminders of this if we possibly can. I think this is the underlying reason why people did not want to hear anything about the fate of the Jews. Horror stories that arouse hatred cause an emotional short circuit that excludes any empathy for the victims. The Attica prison uprising is a case in point. The "liberators" were not interested in the fate of the hostages—rumors of their castration justified the frenzied assault.

False compassion can also facilitate denial of destructive feelings. On March 9, 1983, a court in San Jose, California, found a mother innocent of having murdered her eight-year-old son. The woman, who weighed two hundred pounds, had sat on her son's chest for nearly two hours to punish him for playing with matches and for taking six cents from the kitchen cabinet. Nine days later the boy died from a stroke attributed to suffocation. The court decided that the mother could not be found guilty of showing an unfeeling disregard for life. During the trial, she justified her action by saying that a child guidance counselor had advised her to use her full weight when her son was disobedient. She took this literally and actually sat on him until his ten-year-old sister called the police when she heard him crying for air.[26]

What are we to think of a mother whose empathic feelings are so inaccessible that she is unaware of the consequences of sitting on her son's chest and is not touched by her own child's death cries, to which the boy's sister was able to respond? In the trial, twelve upstanding citizens went along with this perversion of humanity. What interests me here is not the woman's legal guilt but the distortion of human feelings she displayed. This mother claimed to be concerned with raising her son properly, but concealed behind her concern was hatred.

Violence toward children is generally an indication of the presence of artificial feelings. The full extent of violence toward children is just beginning to be recognized today. David Bakan's research on child abuse shows how strongly people deny the existence of something that contradicts their need to believe the myth that everything is all right.[27] David G. Gil found that more than one fifth of adults in the United States, by their own admission, could conceive of harming a child and that 16 percent admitted they sometimes came close to injuring a child.[28]

In 1979, The Year of the Child, Amnesty International reported that children have increasingly become victims of political violence, even on the part of governments. It documented the fate of thirty-five children from twenty-one countries who had been persecuted, imprisoned, tortured, taken from their parents, or executed. It also reported the murder of close to one hundred children by the ruler of the Central African Empire (now the Central African Republic) and the massacre of approximately five thousand children and adolescents between December 1977 and February 1978 in Ethiopia.[29] Violence and cruelty toward children are logical expressions of self-hatred, since those who are weakest and most helpless arouse the greatest rage in adults who have relinquished their autonomy to the greatest degree.

A report on Guatemala reveals that in 1985 the head of state, Gen. Oscar Humberto Mejía Víctores, accused of subversion and persecuted all citizens who took part in trying to locate the "disappeared." A twenty-four-year-old mother named Rosario Godoy de Cuevas, for example, whose husband had been abducted and who had joined a support group of Guatemalan women searching for their missing loved ones, disappeared herself. Her body was later found along with that of her brother and her infant son. The baby's fingernails had been pulled out.[30] In this instance, "patriotism" is used not only to disguise murderous impulses but especially to conceal hatred for children.

The denial of destructive feelings takes countless forms. In 1981, referring to Dachau, whose use as a memorial to the victims of National Socialism he wanted to terminate, Heinrich Wiesner of the Bavarian Ministry of the Interior said, "At some point even Dachau has to become a normal place again."[31] Of course, people who are afraid of suffering use the word "normal" to blot out memory.

On May 1, 1986, following a six-month trial, a federal court in Tucson, Arizona, convicted six leaders of a church-based sanctuary movement of conspiring to smuggle illegal aliens from El Salvador and Guatemala into the United States. Two others were found guilty of transporting and concealing an illegal alien. The defendants included two Catholic priests, a Catholic nun, a Presbyterian minister, and four lay workers. The sanctuary movement started in 1982 when several churches declared publicly that they would provide haven for political refugees from Central America. The movement spread to some three hundred churches and synagogues, over twenty cities, eleven universities, and the states of New Mexico and New York. The Reagan administration, however, considered Salvadorans and Guatemalans illegal aliens rather than refugees seeking political asylum from persecution and torture.[32]

The judge, Earl H. Carroll, played a crucial role in the trial. He shared the view of the United States government that there was no civil war in El Salvador or Guatemala and, hence, that refugees from those countries were merely illegal aliens. Therefore, at pretrial hearings he granted government motions to bar the defense from presenting any testimony that had to do with human rights violations. He also barred the defense from arguing that the actions of the accused were necessary to save human lives, forbade mention of the defendants' religious beliefs and motivations, and also forbade reference to the 1949 Geneva Conventions, the

United Nations Protocol of 1967, and even the U.S. Refugee Act of 1980 concerning the treatment of political refugees. By imposing these restrictions, the judge excluded virtually everything the attorneys planned to present in defense of the accused.[33]

One of the defendants, Sister Darlene, reported in an interview that U.S. immigration authorities had broken into her apartment, confiscated documents, and arrested a twenty-year-old Salvadoran woman living there. "Two of her brothers had been killed by death squads. Her husband had been accidentally shot by a drunken guardsman. She had been forced to flee, leaving two small children behind. . . . I was very frustrated at the trial because I had hoped to testify. I wanted to tell my story. But the Judge would not have allowed me to tell what I saw in Central America, or, for that matter, about my religious and moral convictions concerning sanctuary. My fellow-defendants and I were tried on the simple charge of having aided Salvadoran and Guatemalan refugees who entered this country illegally. We have never denied that. We simply deny that it was a crime for us to do so."[34]

This trial demonstrates how the range of our experience is diminished by the definition of what that experience should be. As a result, empathy is curtailed from the very outset of development. This, in turn, fosters alienation—here under the official auspices of a highly placed representative of the law. Despite such pressures, not everyone can be easily made to go along with inhumane procedures: the jury deliberated for nearly fifty hours before arriving at a verdict.

A verdict handed down by a German court represents an even more grotesque distortion of human feelings. This court, in Lüneburg, decided that Turks had no right to asylum, even though they might face torture upon return to their country. The court based its verdict on the argument that traditional attitudes in Turkey countenanced torture and, furthermore, that torture in that country could be regarded as an ordinary measure on the part of the authorities to ensure national security. Such traditions, the court stated, could not simply be ignored. The Turk seeking asylum in this case was a Kurd—that is, a member of a minority traditionally persecuted in Turkey—who had been imprisoned there many times and had also been tortured.[35] In view of "legal" decisions of this kind, it can come as no surprise that the overall level of humane responsiveness continues to decline.

Since feelings that are not feelings conceal destructiveness behind a facade of moral correctness, they are characterized by an absence of genuine empathy. This lack of empathy takes so many forms that we can easily become confused about our real feelings. In November 1985, a court in Duisberg, Germany, imposed a small fine on five members of a soccer club who had stoned a bus filled with members of a rival soccer club, injuring some of them. The presiding judge said it had not been proved that the five accused had been *conscious* of the life-threatening nature of their actions. The crucial point is that the real motives behind the attackers' "youthful exuberance" were obviously murderous.[36] Here again a judge was practicing dissociation: everyone knows that stones can kill and that anyone throwing stones must have murderous impulses. By ignoring the essential nature of the defendants' actions—by ignoring that which all violent people know in their hearts—the court contributed toward allowing lawbreakers to hold justice in contempt. This is a good example of how representatives of law and order themselves undermine justice.

Feelings that are not feelings can be recognized by the manifold forms of violence they generate. That is also the reason why the world of the "well adjusted" is so unable to curb the violence engulfing it. To get to the roots of violence, one would have to acknowledge that overt violence and the latent violence lurking beneath the surface of conformity have the same origin.

V

Conformity, Rebellion, and Violence

CONFORMITY TO ESTABLISHED values and forms, accompanied by disregard for the inner life, provides a never-ending source of the daily violence surrounding us. As long as success is defined in terms of control and domination and our self-esteem is based on this type of success, the various kinds of social organization under which people live will make little difference: the self will still be impaired. A change in political ideology will neither alter this impaired self nor eliminate the violence for which it is responsible.

Karl Marx envisioned a renewed humanity liberated from helplessness and slavery through a redistribution of the means of production. Together with Friedrich Engels, he analyzed in brilliant detail the economic structure of capitalism and its emphasis on greed and possessions. But he proceeded from the assumption that helplessness is a weakness that human beings must overcome, and he made the conquest of things of the external world—including nature—the supreme human goal. Thus, he perpetuated the ideology of the power-oriented self along with the social evils he thought he was fighting. He gave a new direction to power struggles without changing their source. Worse yet, by dealing with human potential—for morality, for instance—solely in economic terms, he blocked the path to an understanding of the real roots of the drive for power.

Helplessness cannot be overcome by accumulating and exercising power. Any theory that advocates this does violence to individual human beings and their personal histories. When left-wing social theory claims to explain human development from a historical perspective, it does this at the expense of the individual, because it analyzes power wholly in terms of power. This may sound tautological, yet it is at the core of the kind of theory that views people as determined solely by the *power* of economic forces. Georgii Plekhanov, an early leading theoretician and propagandist of Russian socialism, believed he was describing the role of the individual in his analysis of the historical process, but in fact he denied the individual's role in the making of history: "At the present time, human nature can no longer be regarded as the final and most general cause of historical progress: if it is constant, then it cannot explain the extremely changeable course of history; if it is changeable, then obviously its changes are themselves determined by historical progress."[1]

It is not only Marxist theory that denies the importance of the inner world in the interpretation of historical events. Russell Jacoby has pointed out that there is widespread amnesia concerning the significance of the inner life.[2] While Marxism at least makes an attempt at historical analysis, most other economic theories do not even consider human beings in terms of their historical development. Even a Marxist like Louis Althusser proclaimed that "the study of history is not only scientifically but also politically useless."[3] In response to this, the English socialist E. P. Thompson noted that Althusser's dismissal of history made him unable to deal with human experience.[4] And any theory that cannot deal with experience, which is always historical, has lost its reference points in reality.

Where the ideology of power reigns, the self will be cut off from its inner core and thus also from its historical roots—regardless of the specific political form this ideology takes and regardless of who owns the means of production. The resulting destructiveness will find expression either in conformity or rebelliousness.

The Mythology of Maleness and Women's Self-Esteem

Both conformity and rebellion are forms of dependency and have a common source, for if a mother assumes a male point of view, she accepts the male mythology of power and unconsciously initiates those processes leading to either conformity or rebelliousness in her children.

A woman's acceptance of the myth of maleness is an act of self-betrayal. The belief in male superiority is an implicit denial that maternal nurturing can be a basis for self-esteem. It is therefore no surprise that the self-esteem of many women in our culture rests on "masculine" traits unrelated to their own female ability to give birth and to nurture.

John K. Antill and John D. Cunningham suggest that "masculinity" (that is, drive, power, and achievement) is the key factor contributing to self-esteem in women as well as men: "The description of oneself in terms of feminine characteristics is largely irrelevant to males' self-esteem and in females it tends to be linked with low self-esteem"![5] The authors seem to be unaware that the results of their survey of over two hundred college men and women merely reflect our culture's distorted value system in which women see their feminine traits as negative.

In this connection, it is significant—and indicative of male madness—that homosexuality takes entirely different forms among male prisoners than it does among female ones. Women in prison turn to homosexuality to seek closeness, warmth, and security as a way of surviving the loneliness, degradation, and other psychological injuries of incarceration.[6] A study of male prisoners, on the other hand, points out that "males still feel they must demonstrate their masculinity by force: by fighting, sodomizing weaker ones, buying favors, and discharging debts with a sexual 'favor.' However, the persons who are forced to comply, or traffic in sex, are viewed with contempt by those rated as highly masculine." Naturally, these "highly masculine" leaders do *not* consider themselves to be homosexual![7]

These two studies conclusively show that there is a female sense of self-esteem different from that of males. But the women in this instance were not college students. These prisoners had *not* adopted masculine categories: almost 70 percent of them were mothers and had therefore experienced giving life and nurture; most of them had no homosexual experience prior to prison. But where women's self-esteem is patterned after men's, they reject their own value and become contemptuous of their femininity. It may even lead to a woman's feeling contempt for herself because she "*could* be raped by a man," as a female patient once said to me. This is the ultimate expression of female submissiveness. Because she is (or could be) his victim, the woman here subscribes to the man's belief in his superiority and joins in his contempt for women. That is why she ends by hating herself.

For women like this, power will necessarily become the object of their desires. First, it is a compensation essential for the balance of their psychic structure. But since women as a rule are not granted power, they will find "the most obvious source of relief and compensation" in their relations with their children, according to Ronald V. Sampson.[8] Their children become the objects of a bogus affection that manipulates and exploits them. The heart of the matter is that these mothers remain trapped in the mythology of maleness and insist on forcing it on their children. This can happen in two ways. In the first, the mother constantly shows admiration for her child—especially if it is a boy—in order to feel herself strong and powerful via the child. By means of her admiration, she seduces her son into believing that he has an extraordinary importance for her, thereby evoking and continually reinforcing in him a dream of greatness and fame. Since she approves of everything the child does, he will not develop any feeling for right and wrong. In the second, the mother, acting in the name of the father, characteristically insists on the child's submission.

The first route leads to the development of men without the constrictions of conscience. The second, when "successful," leads to conformist behavior that does not seek power itself but wants only to participate in it. In the latter case, guilt feelings play a crucial role.

Samuel Butler, in his novel *The Way of All Flesh* (1903), gives an exact description of a mother who is satisfied with exercising power *over* her children for its own sake (as distinguished from a mother who wants to attain power *through* them). Here, the children's submission is demanded in the name of the father, whom she herself hates but cannot admit to hating. Shortly before the birth of her youngest child, she writes as her testament, in case she should die in childbirth (a classic occasion for imparting guilt feelings!), a letter to her children, admonishing them about their father: ". . . he has devoted his life to you and taught you and laboured to lead you to all that is right and good. Oh, then, be sure that you *are* his comforts. Let him find you obedient, affectionate and attentive to his wishes, upright, self-denying, and diligent; let him never blush for or grieve over the sins and follies of those who owe him such a debt of gratitude. . . ."[9] She passes her own prison on to her children, ensuring that behavior patterns of domination and control will live on as her legacy.

By insisting on a father's authority in order to establish their own position of power, parents of this type are presenting a false facade. And when authority is equated with goodness and nurture, children will experience their parents not as they are but in terms of the images their parents need for their own self-esteem.

This is the prehistory of conformist children. Ann Roskam found that a group of adolescent girls with a great need for achievement and a high degree of conformity inevitably saw their parents as an abstract unit, not as separate beings with gradations of good and bad.[10] Similarly, Helen Bluvol found in a group of achievement-oriented adolescent boys this same inability to differentiate parents as individuals.[11] These conformist teenagers were so cut off from their deepest feelings that they denied, for example, having experiences of anxiety and conflict and even having dreams. The way they experienced themselves as autonomous was through struggling with others—not with themselves. They experienced themselves as "autonomous" when they were able to outdo others!

Roskam also discovered why the girls felt so secure: they avoided everything that was new, different, and unfamiliar. They had a fundamental need to keep their world constant and unambiguous, illustrated by the way they clung to a static image of their parents, whom they saw as mythical, not human, beings. Their inability to see their mother and father as separate individuals was related to their need for security, which forced them to see their parents as they wanted to be seen. They relegated their real experience of their parents to a different psychic sphere.[12] In Bluvol's study, it was the "underachievers," the nonconformists, who defined themselves in terms of their inner self rather than in terms of superiority to others[13] and who were therefore closer to genuine autonomy.

The Good and the Bad Mother

The distortion that results from this can be described as follows: the mother whose bad aspects are actually experienced must be seen as the good mother, because the vision of the truly good mother the child once hoped for is connected with the memory of despair, which is felt as a threat to psychic integrity. Thus, the child has a compulsive need to cling to the myth the parents have created about themselves, since she or he cannot deal with the ambiguity lying in the contradiction between myth and reality.

Conformist children will, as adults, direct their hatred and contempt toward women who demonstrate genuine compassion and nurturing qualities. The split this causes in psychic organization is most clearly visible in those extreme cases of people who torment and torture others. The most violent among them can take sadistic pleasure in torturing women, while at the same time expressing a great reverence for motherhood. Perhaps Klaus Barbie's example, discussed earlier, is surpassed only by the torture of women by the Argentinian junta that ruled with incomparable fiendishness until 1983. Yet "the mothers of the Plaza de Mayo" who demonstrated every Thursday afternoon in front of the government seat in Buenos Aires to protest the disappearance of their sons and daughters were seldom harassed. The same men who raped, tortured and in most cases murdered young women did not touch these mothers.[14]

In this example, the full extent of dissociation is revealed: on the one hand, abstract reverence is paid to mothers and on the other, flesh-and-blood women are hated and violated. This should not be dismissed as an extreme case, for the underlying pattern in conformist development is always the same: the bad mother is glorified as the good mother, and the actual good mother in every woman (as well as the "good mother" in every man) is furiously hated and persecuted. The father in such cases is always the authority, always distant and undefined. Perhaps his unattainability contributes to the unconscious homosexual element in the life of many males who try to conform to the myth of maleness.

A Conformist's Sleight of Hand

In an essay, V. S. Naipaul paints a very accurate portrait of a conformist—a man without too much ambition but with the ability to shape an unambiguous image of the world that he can accept.[15] This portrait was part of Naipaul's coverage of the Republican National Convention of 1984.

E. J. was a thirty-two-year-old man who at personal financial sacrifice was active in Ronald Reagan's reelection campaign. When Naipaul interviewed him, he was working for
the Conservative Alliance on its Human Rights and National
Survival Program. E. J. stated: "Our first aim is to stop communism. *And* turn it back. We feel it shouldn't exist. We feel
all the world should be as free as we are." The organization he
supported, he pointed out, had domestic beginnings, having
been founded to fight liberal legislation. By that E. J. mainly
meant busing, the attempt in the sixties to achieve racial integration in the schools. "Busing brought misery to many families. . . . I know that I was going to private school at the time
and I can remember the desperation of parents—they were
trying to get away from something." He said that his married
sister had also suffered because of it.[16]

When E. J. speaks of desperation and misery here, then it
is only to seek sympathy for his refusal to take responsibility for the fate of a group of underprivileged fellow
citizens who experience discrimination. There is a total
absence of empathy for the plight of others, and self-pity is
meant to divert attention from this lack and justify it. The
absence of feeling is turned into "feeling" by a sleight of
hand, and in this way, others are supposed to be won over.
In fact, this happened to a colleague of Naipaul's at the
convention who was very moved by E. J.'s "desperation,"
even though he did not share his politics.[17] Self-pity is
indeed often taken for genuine feeling, and therefore the
fact that one's intentions are evil goes unnoticed. Thus, the
real situation is turned into its opposite. The motives of
those who want to help the truly desperate become suspect
because the hysterically narrowed perception of one's own
"pain" draws all attention to itself.

While proclaiming his adherence to Christianity, in the
same breath E. J. repudiated Christian compassion: "I belong [*sic*] to the Episcopalian Church myself. It's one of the
mainline churches in the United States, but I left it. I left it
because when I went there I did not hear religion. I heard our

priest rail against our government and the injustices of our society and Vietnam. . . . I left the church . . . because my priest had decided that religion had to become a social movement."[18] E. J. was unaware that all religions begin as social movements. When in the course of their development, churches begin to support the status quo, those members of the clergy who want to restore to the churches their original mission inevitably become "a nuisance." What is even more disconcerting about this young man's criticism of the Church is his reproach that helping one's neighbor (one of the goals of the priest he attacked) would destroy one's peace of mind. This is an example of how people can renounce at a single stroke all feelings of compassion and at the same time appear sensitive.

In a similar way, a little boy can react to accusations of heartlessness by crying, "Look at what you're doing to me," successfully diverting attention from the reason he was reproached. This is how a basic distortion starts: when mothers and fathers in a situation like this respond to false self-pity with kindness in order to make themselves feel understanding and generous and thereby raise their self-esteem, they are teaching their child deception. The trick of how to win others over is thus learned at an early age: one appeals to others' subliminal feeling of guilt and releases them from it by allowing oneself to be pitied. We all have used this trick— the self-serving lie—at some point in our lives.

We must keep in mind that conformists hate the good and love the bad. This basic attitude arises from their need to defend the bad mother as good. They must deny the validity of every good cause and invest their energies in social ideologies that distort their perception. This is part of a continuing attempt not to see their mothers as they once actually did perceive them. When they are faced with the danger of having to expand their consciousness, conformists invariably react with self-pity. This saves them from having to confront their fear of the truth.

That the distortion of the good as bad and the bad as good

is a widespread characteristic of conformists is shown by their way of dealing with their own pasts. E. J. emphasized how proud he was of his father because he had worked his way up from poverty to become the best doctor possible. But poverty does not evoke compassion in E. J.; it is something that must be rejected. "It was instilled from birth that anybody could do anything in the world they wished, that if they had the desire and the will there was nothing to stop them. That was the beauty of America. I can remember other neighbors' kids getting in trouble for different things and getting spanked. The worst thing anyone in our family could do was *not doing our best*, whether it was cutting the grass or studying at school." That is the only thing he got spanked for. "In 1967 ... [m]y father was opposed to what the government was doing. He felt our government was creating a welfare state, which he said is a mild way of saying 'socialistic.' On top of that he felt our government was backing down to the communists. He believed that the communists fully planned to take over the entire world."[19]

One's own pain and the suffering of others are dismissed by submitting to parental dictates. Yet the death-orientation caused by the sacrifice of autonomy is, of course, denied. Thus, E. J.'s father died at the age of fifty-seven from "overwork," which was considered a distinction. He never saw his neighbors' trouble or misfortune but only their threat to his own existence. In such families, one's own heart is the enemy within, and it is projected outward onto the evil do-gooders who want to deprive them of what they have worked so hard for. " 'That story of poverty and struggle is something many people of the Right tell,' " Naipaul quotes his colleague as saying.[20] Suffering does not arouse compassion, however, but only self-pity as a way of avoiding love. The bad mother, who spanked one because one wanted something other than what she thought was best, is idealized as the good mother. The longing for a truly good mother remains but is feared as something dangerous.

A Terrorist of the Right

The confessions of Stefan, a twenty-two-year-old German terrorist of the radical Right, are reported by his contemporary Giovanni di Lorenzo.[21] Stefan provides a shocking example of how basic the reversal and denial of one's own history is in the development of the conformist personality. His story shows the way acceptance of the Basic Lie about love makes a person incapable of independent thought and feeling. Stefan demonstrates how destructiveness within spills over into open violence and how the whole process takes place under the guise of a commitment to morality and decency.

This violence goes hand in hand with fear of change, a fear that also characterizes nonviolent, well-adjusted citizens. This is why the latter are so willing to "employ" violent terrorists for the sake of maintaining order. "There are, of course, in every society," writes the warden of a British prison, "sick and perverted men and women who would gladly spend their lives as professional punishers, degraders, humiliators, hurters, torturers and killers of their fellow men—people who are fulfilled by psychological and physical violence against others. They exist in every society. But when any society legitimizes their perversion by employing them in numbers to degrade, and punish, and destroy, that society itself is sick unto death."[22] In Stefan's case, for example, because the police did not intervene when his group attacked leftists, its members felt that they were working for the police.[23]

One of the remarkable things about Stefan is the way he contradicts himself; much of what he says is inconsistent, but he apparently is unaware of this. It is because we so often overlook these contradictions that we have difficulty recognizing the true nature of people like him. Stefan reports:

> My parents love us [Stefan and his brother] above everything. . . . We never talked about our troubles, or only when it was already too late. We never got close. . . .[24]

I believe I unconsciously hold it against my father that he never made a career for himself although he is highly intelligent. . . .[25]

My parents made mistakes, a real problem. Why and what they were I don't know exactly. I can't remember there ever being any tenderness between me and my parents. I think they were quite inhibited in such things. My parents never understood us kids either. They never caught on if I did something wrong . . . I was never physically punished in my life.[26]

Stefan displays feelings in these words but no awareness of the contradictions in them. He can proudly say, "My parents love us above everything," and, in the same breath, deny any tenderness on their part. He uses words for their effect, yet without any relationship to inner realities.

I looked for approval by belonging to a tough and very masculine group. . . . When I thought about National Socialism, the first thing that occurred to me was the old personalities from that time: the Führer, the whole movement, good German soldiers, the toughness, the community. There was this slogan that fascinated me: "One people, one nation, one Führer." All those atrocities that were supposed to have happened in the Nazi period, we always denied them. All the rightists I was with always said the Nazi crimes never happened. They really believed that. But at the same time, as a result of their complexes, they thought things like the brutality of rubber truncheons and toughness were good. Whenever we got into a fight and told a Commie you're going to be put in a concentration camp, then we really meant it. . . . We never denied that the Jews were interned under Hitler, but we don't believe they were systematically exterminated. . . .[27]

I began the new year with hanging out and getting into trouble. The beginning of February, just before graduating, I dropped out of school. . . . A few days later I was arrested for robbery. Just don't remind me of that story. I still get a bad conscience. How would you feel if you assaulted an elderly woman? But the whole thing was unintentional. . . . They didn't catch us until we tried to cash a forged check at a bank. Somehow I just mustn't think about it. . . .[28]

It's something of a comfort that we only have another fifty years to live. Material things have great value for me. For me they mean more freedom. . . . Yes, money is primarily freedom. Work is the unpleasant side of life, what you're forced to do. . . . I'm not a believer. . . . Maybe I've only believed in God when I wanted something from him. . . .[29]

I'm pretty satisfied with my looks. I mean, they're okay. I look in the mirror a lot. . . . I have my own style. Only sometimes I think of myself as simply too soft. I'd like to be more masculine. . . .[30]

When you get right down to it, humanity is bad and egotistic. . . . My friends and I stick together and shut out the rest of the world. Friendship is the highest value in life. If I had to characterize my friends, I'd say there are three types: rich ones, petty criminals, and drug freaks. . . . [My friend] still lives with his family. They really worship him, he's the man in the house. He runs around at home with a bare chest, and they really admire him. . . . Sometimes he lets women support him. Then he takes everything they have from them, and then he takes off. He really acts like a pig toward them. . . . For me, a man who doesn't cheat on a woman isn't a real man. Somehow, women are always looking for a strong man. . . . I'm past the age when women meant something important for me. . . . Naturally, I'm very dependent on women in a way. But that's nothing except the sex drive. A good friendship among men is worth more than any girl. . . .[31]

The idea of family doesn't mean much to me. . . . When I look back on my development, I see why it was more likely that I would join a rightist group. Maybe I could have landed in a leftist group instead, but probably our whole upbringing has made the Right more appealing to us. It starts with the way you dress. Our ideology stresses that we should be clean, fresh, and proper. Those who look different are automatically scum.[32]

Stefan's self-pity and his need to be proper are what lend the contradictions in his statements a certain coherence. At the core of these contradictions is the love-hate generated by parents who lack any feeling for their children's needs. These children become very dependent on parental care but at the same time try to bite the hand they want to be fed by. In later life, this form of exploiting others—for example, women— gives them an illusion of freedom. And everything that re- minds them of the truth arouses their desire for revenge, so they inflict violence on a world that does not correspond completely to their dissociated state. But all this takes place in the name of love, love for the bad mother, who must be defended as good. The truly good mother, or everything reminiscent of her, arouses derisive hatred, for she reminds them of the deep, genuine needs and longings that the real mother once awakened but did not fulfill and that therefore must now be killed.

War and Rebellion

The process of killing one's own real needs under the banner of protecting love and purity has been one of the driving forces of history, if by history we mean a series of wars and upheavals. Norman Cohn's book *Pursuit of the Millennium*, a brilliant analysis of revolutionary messianism in the Middle Ages, describes this process. He depicts people who, in expec- tation of the Millennium and Christ's earthly reign, waged a bitter battle for a future life of peace and happiness.[33] Yet salvation seemed to be unattainable. They could not slay the enemy whom they pursued with hatred and violence. They sought this enemy exclusively outside themselves and, there- fore, were unable to find the real—the inner—enemy. And so they ended by fighting only for the sake of fighting and de- struction. Their yearning for salvation turned into boundless rage and an untiring vengefulness against an abstract external enemy devoid of all human attributes. Every battle became the hunt for an enemy.

Wars become necessary when people lose the ability to see

other people as human beings. When the true enemy—the bad mother—cannot be acknowledged, then as an adult the child must project the counter-image of the bad mother, namely the good mother as the bad one. As adults such children defend the bad mother as good by persecuting those who remind them of the promise of a good mother. The good mother and everyone representing her become the enemy by virtue of threatening to reawaken the earlier needs for genuine love, which would jeopardize the image of the mother with whom they once made a compromise. By means of war, one defends the cohesion of a self that has decisively divorced itself from the need for genuine love.

Of course, outer events play a role in this process. As Cohn shows, during the Middle Ages the breakdown of the social and economic orders led to a loss of meaning for the individual.[34] That is the crux of the matter: a self based on dissociation can no longer maintain cohesion when threatened by social upheavals. If the social structure begins to crumble, people's pent-up rage erupts. Then murderous impulses and inner chaos, which can be channeled only by means of an external "enemy," become visible.

It is a characteristic of selves of this kind that they can just as quickly become "sane" again when the authority of the social order appears reestablished. This explains the apparent paradox of a Russian army that in the years 1905 and 1906 repeatedly mutinied, as well as put down rebellions. As John Bushnell describes it, the same soldiers behaved in radically different ways in rapid succession and in ten months went through two complete cycles of rebellion and renewed loyalty. Troops that put down rebellions from January to October 1905 mutinied from the end of October to the beginning of December, and by the end of December they were again shooting at civilians, only to rebel anew from May to June of 1906 and at the end of July to suppress uprisings again.[35]

Bushnell shows that the soldiers' fluctuating behavior had

nothing to do with their treatment or with their political views. All that mattered was how they perceived the regime's authority—that alone influenced the stability of their sense of self. If they believed the old regime was coming to an end, they mutinied, but if they believed it was still in control, they repressed civilians.[36]

We see here that it is not so much the disintegration of an external social structure that produces rebellion but whether there is still an authority to whom one can submit. If it no longer seems to be there, then a personality that has been based on conformity falls apart. And thus shifts of loyalty occur—in this case repeatedly. The ever-present readiness for violence turns directly against what was formerly considered good.

Naturally, this could also be interpreted as throwing off the chains of one's earlier adaptation to something bad that one considered good—the old regime. But a non-autonomous self does not revolt because it has undergone a fundamental transformation; it simply changes the target of its violence. Revolutions may or may not change the forms servitude takes; in fact, they do not affect servitude at all as long as obedience to authority is not overcome. The bad will go on being defended as good, and no true liberation of the self will take place. Yet that alone would lead one back to the true need for love and break the vicious circle of destructiveness.

To return to the Middle Ages: in his book, Norman Cohn describes the medieval eschatological expectations and the growing hope for the coming of a warrior messiah who would save the downtrodden from unbearable oppression.[37]

Poverty, wars, and local famines were so much a part of normal life that they were taken for granted and could therefore be faced in a sober and realistic manner. But when a situation arose which was not only menacing but went altogether outside the normal run of experience, when people

were confronted with hazards which were all the more frightening because they were unfamiliar—at such times a collective flight into the world of phantasies could occur very
easily. . . . Thus when the Black Death reached western Europe in 1348 it was at once concluded that some class of
people must have introduced [a poison] into the water-
supply. . . .[38]

At that point, the search for a savior reached explosive pro-
portions: "Those who attached themselves to such a saviour
saw themselves as a holy people—and holy just because of
their unqualified submission to the saviour. . . . They were
his good children and as a reward they shared in his supernatural power. . . . [A]nd meanwhile their every deed,
though it were robbery or rape or massacre, not only was
guiltless but was a holy act."[39]

We have revolt here, but it simply expresses what under-
lies every act of submission: the longing for salvation
through identification with authority. And revolt gives free
rein to hatred. Destruction can be presented as a good act
without one having to recognize or confront the Basic Lie.
The fact that in warfare the external enemy is almost always
a man reinforces the oedipal aspect of the defense of the
mother. This makes it even more difficult to uncover the Lie.
Although the external enemy represents the bad father, this
bad father corresponds in fact to the image the mother had of
him and not to the real father. The mother hated and/or
feared this image because it was all-powerful, superhuman,
and evil, whereas the real father, although authoritarian,
was weak. The "good" father is thus not the one who helps
one find one's own self but he who spares one inner conflict.
He is the father who gives one permission to vent destructiveness, who releases one from struggling with one's conscience. In other words, the "good" father is the bad father,
who completely destroys the remnants of the really good
mother. This means that fear not love reigns supreme.

The Rebel and the Conformist

What about the rebel who in word and deed repudiates all forms of conformity? He searches for something better, for a link with humanity, asserts his difference in order not to give even the slightest appearance of conforming—yet here too violence rears its head. How then do we explain the rebel?

Henry Miller, a great rebel himself, writes in his study of Rimbaud, *The Time of the Assassins*, that all rebelliousness derives from "the search for one's true link with humanity. . . . [The rebel] has to establish the ultimate difference of his own peculiar being and [in] doing so discover his kinship with all humanity, even the very lowest. Acceptance is the key word. But acceptance is precisely the great stumbling block. It has to be total acceptance and not conformity."[40]

Yet establishing one's difference leads to "play[ing] out every facet of one's being." One becomes trapped and never stops finding reasons to complain and, therefore, new reasons to rebel. This kind of search for freedom "does not take into account other people's differences, only one's own. It will never aid one to find one's link, one's communion, with all mankind. One remains forever separate, forever isolate."[41]

Henry Miller provides us with a powerful insight:

All this has but one meaning for me—that one is still bound to the mother. All one's rebellion was but dust in the eye, the frantic attempt to conceal this bondage. Men of this stamp are always against their native land—impossible to be otherwise. Enslavement is the great bugaboo, whether it be to country, church or society. Their lives are spent in breaking fetters, but the secret bondage gnaws at their vitals and gives them no rest. They must come to terms with the mother before they can rid themselves of the obsession of fetters. "Outside! Forever outside! Sitting on the doorstep of the mother's womb.". . . No wonder one is alienated from the mother. One does not notice her, except as an obstacle. One wants the comfort and security of her womb, that darkness and ease which for the unborn is the equivalent of illumination and acceptance for the truly born. . . . One may be acclaimed as a great rebel, but one will never be loved. And for the rebel above all men it is necessary to know love, to give it even more than to receive it, and to be it even more than to give it.[42]

Yet Miller continues, "He is a traitor at heart because he fears the humanity in him which would unite him with his fellow man. . . ."[43] Miller makes the point that lurking in every rebel is the fear of a mother who might devour him, use him, exploit him. This makes him the opposite of the conformist, who pays lip service to loving his mother while hating all womanhood.

The rebel distances himself from feelings because he fears the love he is seeking. The conformist, on the other hand, hates love because otherwise he would have to acknowledge that his mother never loved him. Both are cut off from love, and both avoid it. The rebel claims he can do without it, while the conformist claims that he received it, but both end up dependent: the conformist by expecting to be rewarded for proper behavior, the rebel by taking (but not admitting that he is doing so) because what he was given was never enough. What distinguishes the two types is that the rebel insists that the promises of the good mother be kept, whereas the conformist persists in seeking recognition from the bad mother. The rebel does not want to admit that the promises of the good mother and his experience of the bad mother have something to do with each other. Like the conformist, he overlooks having experienced the mother as bad *and* good.

Yet the possibility of authenticity resides in rebellion, not in conformity. In the search for the good mother lies the longing for a loving link with humanity. But how can the rebel find this link if he, like the conformist, has cut off access to his own helplessness? Both have experienced injured feelings, and both protect themselves by relinquishing their feelings—with a crucial difference: the conformist in addition denies his loss of feeling by calling "good" something that is bad.

The following case history illustrates the nature of the injury suffered by rebels as well as the turning point in their development that distinguishes them from conformists. Paula came to see me during the summer of 1984; she was nineteen, with the face of a madonna and a punk hairstyle. She belonged to the "cool" generation, called herself a revolutionary, and had taken part in demonstrations in several European cities. Her parents were wealthy, successful lawyers who belonged to the upper class. Paula was all intellect and showed no signs of warmth, just rage and stubborn demands. Although she totally rejected the state, she insisted that it support her. She could so impress people with her sharp intelligence that a couple who had given her a ride lent her the key to their weekend place. Now, however, as she sat across from me, she had nothing but contempt for these people and their house. She was unable to experience gratitude, did not want to feel "obligated." Feelings were a trap for her: to give in to feelings meant having to meet authority's expectations for conformity.

That is the background of the hidden injury to Paula and so many members of her generation. She was wounded by parents who tried to buy her love. She protected herself by distancing herself from her feelings as much as possible. That way she was invulnerable. It became clear to me that Paula's parents treated her like an advertisement for themselves, like their trademark, so to speak. They loved her because she confirmed their image of themselves as good parents; they did not love her for herself. They gave Paula everything but only in order to make her their own compliant property.

By having as little feeling as possible, children can defend themselves against this kind of nonpunitive manipulation that denies the violence of its possessiveness. They turn away from what threatens them: their need to love and be loved. That is why Paula and her generation defend themselves so vigorously against those who have made them dependent, and they think they are above it all when they keep on demanding more. Thus, they do not need to be grateful or to be aware of their dependence. They have submitted in part to their parents' unspoken ideology: "We will take care of you, but you must be exactly the way we want you to be." Consequently, they behave dependently, but in order to be able to live with their dependency they refuse to be grateful. That is the only way they can live with the insincerity of their parents' love.

This leads to a further injury, however: they must not acknowledge their need for love, for then they would be vulnerable. Conformists, too, experience this injury, but they know how to make it appear as though they were in harmony with their needs. They can then play the role of a loving human being without really feeling any love at all. The rebels, on the other hand, maintain a fictitious invulnerability by acting as though they had no such needs. Both demand to be taken care of—the conformist, as pointed out, for good behavior; the rebel in order to prove that the world cannot give him or her enough. Both suffer from an inability to feel, although we tend not to notice this in the conformist's case because of that person's ability to give the opposite impression.

The Terrorist

One of the most extreme forms of dependence is revealed in the new terrorism. Its ideological superstructure conceals underlying rage and infantile dependency. As early as 1920, Lenin called ultra-left-wing extremism an infantile disorder that rationalizes impatience with ideological arguments.[44] If we remove the ideological cover, we will notice the vengeful cry of the child, "I want it, and I want it right now." This weapon is forged in homes where everything is available except the one thing that really matters: genuine love.

The denial of dependency has produced a terrorism in

which the act of killing has lost all connection to human experience. Murder becomes a symbolic protest in which the victim has no personal significance. The inability to feel (caused by early injury) is continually reinforced in a spiraling self-alienation. The terrorists devote their entire attention to the mechanics of planning and procedure, so that the act of murder loses all touch with the last vestiges of feeling. Any consciousness of the murderous nature of their deeds is suppressed. In this way, terrorists become as unreachable as the world that has created them. The horror of their situation is not apparent to them.

The German terrorist Bommi Baumann diagnosed this situation accurately: "Your choosing terrorism is already psychologically preprogrammed. I can see it today in my case, it was simply fear of love ... from which you take refuge in an absolute power. If I had really checked out love ahead of time, I wouldn't [have become a terrorist]."[45] To face his fear would have meant confronting the horrors of his early childhood trauma; most people like Bommi do not have the strength to do this and, therefore, keep repeating what has been done to them, but in ways that conceal the real reasons behind their actions.

Underneath lies an abysmal self-rejection (all too often hidden beneath provocative behavior) because one never felt loved. Paula, for example, admitted that she could not stand herself and could not imagine that anyone could ever really like her. The wish to be loved for oneself by parents who did not love their *own* real self is the secret bondage of which Henry Miller speaks.

I recall a young Austrian psychology student who had joined our hiking group on an outing in the Swiss Alps. After we had reached the foot of a glacier, she suddenly ran ahead, approached the edge of the glacier, and disappeared among the gigantic pillars of ice. We could neither see nor hear her, and the situation was quite dangerous, for ice was cracking on all sides, breaking off with a great noise and falling from the glacier's edge. To our great relief, she suddenly appeared again. She told us that she had been driven by an inexplicable urge to find an ice pillar and embrace it. When she found a suitable one, she put her arms around it and held it for a long time. She said she had no idea why. Later, when she told me about her mother, who had avoided all bodily contact with her in her first two years of life, I understood that she was searching for her ice-cold mother among those pillars. She wanted to warm her mother even at the risk of her own death.

Again and again, in our search for a love that was never there, we pursue self-destruction. We believe love to be in the very place where we cannot possibly have it. In this way, we repeat the original rejection and keep proving to ourselves that nothing can come our way. And then, if real love should someday cross our path, we reject it, for who could love us when we are so inadequate?

Paula clings to her parents, especially her father, at the same time trying to hurt them in every conceivable way. Her favorite garment is a pajama top of her father's, yet she has initiated legal proceedings against him for nonsupport. She wants to overturn the structures of a hypocritical society, yet she holds fast to the foundation of this society: the splitting apart of feeling. The ensuing rage makes her cling to those who are the cause of her predicament, although she does not realize she is doing it. Her actions are aimed at forcing her parents to take care of her—on her terms, of course. But it was the very excess of material care that smothered her real needs in the first place. Her parents fostered artificial needs and satisfied them with things money could buy instead of providing the love she actually needed.

The result is that Paula is unable to love, which she herself realizes. She is unable to build a life of her own. Only her rage makes her feel alive. All that distinguishes her from her parents is that they hide their destructive rage behind a facade of correctness. Their attempt to raise a successful daughter in a society that measures everyone's value in terms of success has caused them to murder their daughter's soul.

Paula told me once about a conversation she had with her mother when she was twelve. Her mother was then in therapy and thought it was time to speak "openly" with her daughter. She confided to her that she had never been able to bear it when Paula was cheerful and happy. The therapist had recommended this "frankness," but it was really a way for the mother to avoid confronting her own truth and her own mistakes. All she achieved by it was to wound her daughter even more. This "open" conversation was a way of trying to win Paula's compassion for the fact that her mother hated her.

This created an impossible situation for the twelve-year-old girl. How could she have pity for a mother whose love she still needed? If Paula had stood by her mother, it would have meant sharing in the mother's hatred for her daughter. Feeling for her and with her would have meant Paula accepted the accusation that she was unlovable. And so she had no choice but to suppress all feeling and compassion from then on and rely solely on her intellect.

If her mother had been honest with herself, she would have seen that she would have to live with her mistakes. Instead, she burdened Paula with them in order to free herself of guilt feelings. She seemed to ask for forgiveness, but actually she only revealed her own destructiveness. For a real change to take place, she would have had to recognize that her attempts to achieve a false security were leading to destructiveness. With her "sincerity" she evaded this insight.

Rebellion represents an attempt to throw off the chains of the past. When the rebel loses contact with his heart, however, the rebellion merely perpetuates the old disease in new forms. The difficulty is that a renewal of love is impossible without rebellion. If one never rebels, one never even has a chance to live one's own self. The rebel needs teachers, but as Henry Miller points out, he lacks the patience to listen. Because he is so intent on asserting himself, he will not discover that unrestrained self-assertion is not freedom. He is afraid of acceptance, because he thinks that means self-surrender (whereas true acceptance of another person does not require that person's surrender at all). Although the rebel's deepest wish is to surrender to his mother, he keeps on struggling against this wish, and therefore true acceptance is not possible. This is the truth that remains hidden from the rebel as well as the conformist because they both long for the mother they cannot have in reality.

One is afraid of acceptance because one fears that will mean losing oneself, for in the deepest recesses of one's soul, one seeks deliverance from the pain of rejection by wishing to merge with the mother forever. To accept other people means to see them as they really are without needing to lose oneself in them. It is the unconscious wish to lose oneself that destroys a person. In order to escape this, the conformist never accepts responsibility for his actions but instead allies himself with people with power, thereby remaining "free" to vent his pent-up desire for revenge. The rebel, on the other hand, claims to be different and accepts responsibility for this, but never recognizes that he is thereby only trying to prove to himself that he is *not* dependent on the mother (or father) to whom he so wants to submit. That is what Henry Miller means when he says the rebel fears "the humanity in him which would unite him with his fellow man."[46] If we could help him to stop fearing his love for the good mother, which is primarily a consequence of the promises of the bad mother, then the vicious circle that produces ever new forms of tyranny could be broken.

But until that happens, we must keep Paolo Freire's observation in mind: "The oppressed, having internalized the image of the oppressor ... are fearful of freedom. Freedom would require them to eject this image and replace it with autonomy and responsibility."[47] We must also remember that this internalization is kept alive by the need of the oppressed to ally themselves with those who keep them at a distance.

The extent to which rebels are secretly attracted to the powers they try to resist is documented by many of their own statements. The German writer Peter Schneider published his correspondence with Peter-Jürgen Boock, an imprisoned member of the R.A.F., the German left-wing terrorist organization. In his letters, Boock writes poignantly about how he gradually came to see the insanity of a strategy of violence. He describes the way an individual, once having accepted the ideological consensus of the group, "loses with breathtaking speed the ability to speak and think on his own and, finally, to perceive things independently."[48] Submission to a higher power is then complete. The crucial point is that the rebel has the desire to submit from the very beginning, before joining a group. This desire gives rise to both the rebellion and the loss of self against which he or she originally rebelled.

Boock is one of those rare terrorists who, because he is unable to escape his own empathic perceptions, confronts the murderous nature of his actions. As he was observing the people in an office building during preparations for a terrorist attack, they suddenly became real human beings for him: "[M]y scruples, till then subliminal, began to take on increasingly concrete form. I saw secretaries, Justice Department employees, people young and old, who could have been working there or might be chance visitors. I can remember that I noticed feeling as though a block of ice were growing inside me. . . . What I was now doing had no connection at all with my motivation for joining the R.A.F.; [it] would only produce more senseless victims, aggravate the situation, and make me into a murderer."[49]

Here I should like to stop and take a look at conformist thinking as represented by those in authority. The insights expressed by Peter-Jürgen Boock and Bommi Baumann could be of help in dealing with leftist terrorism. One would assume the government would welcome publication of what they have to say, but that is not the case. Conformist thinking is not concerned with understanding anything, as Heinrich Böll bitterly remarks in connection with the West German government's confiscation of Baumann's book *Terror or Love?*[50] It cannot tolerate thoughts that imply any other motives for action than those that preserve power. And so the German government would hear nothing of Boock's repentance; only if he were to collaborate by betraying his former comrades would they accept his change of mind.

Conformist thinking is self-defeating because it knows only the categories of punishment and submission, but not the potential that lies in understanding. The image of the enemy must be maintained at all costs; for this reason, the "enemy" must never be humanized. Both the revolutionary and the conformist depend on the image of the enemy; they need it in order to rationalize their violence, and they need violence to maintain their positions. Thus, they both will continue in their efforts to provoke violence on the part of their enemy.

To return to terrorism: the abstract quality of its thought reinforces the psychological detachment of its adherents. The use of ideological formulas naturally contributes to this detachment. Antonio Negri, formerly professor of political science at the University of Padua and subsequently one of the spokesmen for Italian radicals of the Left, writes in his book *Sabotage*: "I feel the immediate warmth of the community of workers and proletarians every time I pull the *passamontagna* [the hood that leaves just a slit for the eyes] over my head. . . . When we are successful, I feel joy and happiness: every act of sabotage and destruction overwhelms me as a sign of class solidarity. Nor does the possible risk bother me; it fills me with the feverish emotion of someone awaiting his beloved."[51] What we detect in such statements is not only the transformation of rage into sexuality but also the equation of love with death and destruction. With these orgiastic concepts, the writer removes himself, and presumably his readers as well, from the real consequences his murderous acts have for other human beings. By means of this transformation, the murderer completely loses any feeling of responsibility.

How is this different from General Millán's fiery shout, "Long live Death!"? This glorification of death is another aspect of terrorism that the Left and Right have in common. But I should like to call attention to several other points. Negri was obviously aroused by the element of risk per se. This is reminiscent of one of the revolutionaries in Dostoevsky's novel *The Possessed*, who would rather risk everything than remain in uncertainty. Uncertainty causes fear, and fear makes us very ready to take risks. Negri romanticizes and sexualizes risk in order to conceal his fear. By masking it, he is supporting the myth of male strength, which denies such a feeling. How, then, is he different from his enemies?

Negri's enthusiasm for the warmth of the proletarian community of workers reveals *his* need for warmth; it is a projection he shares with all those intellectuals who know nothing of the reality of working-class life. Although he and the many intellectuals who, like him, are victims of this fiction admire George Orwell, they do not appear to be familiar with his book *The Road to Wigan Pier* (1937) and the many other literary documents that describe proletarian life without romanticizing it. The intellectuals themselves are unaware of their need for warmth, which is disguised by romantic projections. Thus, Negri can enthuse about warmth as a human attribute yet at the same time do everything in his power to destroy it. The one thing that this kind of ideological writing makes clear is that terrorists, too, desire death, because they mistrust and hate life itself.

Violence without Ideology

The general destructiveness all around us is especially visible in the increasing violence at sporting events. This, too, expresses the addiction to the mythology of maleness that makes men hate themselves.

The first outbreak of public violence during a soccer game

to occur after the Second World War was in England in March 1946. The result: thirty-three dead, five hundred injured. This was clearly the forerunner of an international phenomenon. April 1961: five dead and over three hundred injured after a game between Chile and Brazil in Santiago; March 1966: three hundred injured at a soccer game in Cairo; September 1967: forty-four dead and six hundred wounded in Turkey; March 1975: twenty dead in Moscow; September 1979: twelve children trampled to death in Medan, Indonesia; May 1985: a riot after a game between China and Hong Kong in Beijing; May 1985: thirty-nine dead, ten severely injured, two hundred less severely, at a soccer game between England and Italy in Brussels.[52]

In Europe, it is English soccer fans who seem to have played an especially large role in this development, and, therefore, they have been written about the most. Outbreaks of soccer-related violence in England date back to the period between 1885 and the First World War. The ebb and flow of incidents has coincided closely with changes within the English working class. In times of relative affluence, when the values and aspirations of the workers approximated those of the ruling class, violence subsided.[53] However, with the growing division of workers into a comfortable majority and a hard-core minority of unemployed who have no chance of finding work, the problem of riots at soccer games has worsened enormously, especially since the 1960s.

It is not unemployment alone that is involved here, although the outbreaks of violence are a means by which the participants drown out the desperateness of their situation. They do not raise a row to call attention to their situation but to hide their despair. This is illustrated by Wilfried Kratz's report in *Die Zeit* of April 26, 1985, on unemployed youth in Kirkby near Liverpool: "These young people speak with a remarkable cheerfulness, a kind of gallows humor, about their lives. There is no detectable bitterness. It is as though— along with the will to look for a job—criticism, opposition, and the longing for a radical change in existing conditions had disappeared."[54]

Kratz interviewed three young men in a pub and asked them what they had been doing over the past years. " 'Nothing, there's no work in Kirkby,' one of them said with self-assurance. His friend announced with feigned solemnity, 'I have withdrawn from the job market.' All three were living from unemployment benefits. Young people such as these are counted by social workers among 'the lost,' who have never had a job, have no connection to the working world and in fact can no longer be won over to it. They have sunk to the bottom of society."[55]

Michael Harrington noted similar findings back in 1964 when he wrote about young Americans without jobs: "They were restless, shadow-boxing, given to bursts of laughter and comment—energetic like adolescents generally. . . . In this persona, their talk was of girls, drinking, fighting, the life of the streets. . . . [They were] filling up their futureless spare time with a desperate, aimless sensualism, living by petty crime and headed nowhere. . . . They had failed in school, not out of a lack of ability, but because there had been no money at home, no space, no possibility of study. They, in their late teens, were already victims."[56] An English policeman said of their contemporary English counterparts: "All that's left to them is to turn one another on by talking about sex and to brag to one another about how big and strong they are. They're all just young fellows desperately trying to be men."[57]

The decisive point is that these adolescents have submitted wholly to the official ideology of masculine strength. They are victims of the ideology of those who dominate and oppress them, and by idealizing power and violence, they themselves contribute to perpetuating that ideology. Even though their actions appear to be rebellious, in the depths of their being they are conformists. Thus, aimless rebelliousness is the only way they can deal with their predicament.

In order to understand these rowdies, we must place the

concept of adaptation in a broader context than usual. Conformity is reflected not only in "nice" social behavior but also in those situations in which all feelings, with the exception of murderous rage, have been killed. The scorn and contempt for social rules on the part of these adolescents merely conceal the extent to which they have fallen into the trap of conformity, for with their violent behavior, they are merely expressing their acceptance of power as the only reality to be taken seriously.

When I define conformity as denoting murderousness and the death of humane feelings, I am by no means exaggerating. For this applies even to the "nicest" among us. How would one classify the *Challenger* disaster in 1985 in which its entire crew was lost? The commission investigating the tragedy hit the nail on the head when it concluded that an obsession with success resulted in assigning a minor role to the concern for human safety.[58] The question arises: what is the difference between unfeeling rowdies and those in the space program who felt responsible for the technical success of a space voyage but not for the lives of their fellow human beings? True, the expression of violence on the part of the rowdies is more open and direct; they make visible what is camouflaged in the case of top-level decision makers: success is all-important and is part of an ideology in which human concerns do not count.

The fact is that the dynamics are the same; only the manifestations are different, since the "successful" in our society can "sublimate" their murderous intentions so that we do not see them. As Bertolt Brecht writes in *The Threepenny Opera*:

> *For some are in the darkness*
> *And others in the light.*
> *And we see those in the light,*
> *Those in darkness we don't see.*[59]

It is psychology's task to cast light on what we want to keep concealed.

Soccer rowdies are not the only ones committing acts of violence "without ideology." Everywhere we find signs of an increase in self-hatred and, in its wake, a violence that is dissociated from its origins in the human psyche. We need only to open the newspaper and read items from all over the world:

Zuger Tageblatt (Switzerland), December 5, 1979: "At a concert given by the British pop group The Who held in the American city of Cincinnati, eleven young people were killed. They were victims of mass hysteria that broke out when a wild crowd tried to get to the best seats in the city's coliseum. Some of the victims simply were trampled down, the others suffocated. . . . 'They were willing to kill people in order to be able to see well at the concert,' an eyewitness is quoted as saying. 'They just didn't care what happened.' "

Luzerner Tageblatt (Switzerland), September 20, 1980: "Brenda Spencer (fifteen), a schoolgirl from San Diego, California, U.S.A., was given a very special birthday present by her father: a rifle with a telescopic lens. After her father went to work, the girl opened a window in her parents' home and aimed the rifle at the school grounds of the Patrick Henry Junior High School in the suburb of San Carlos. The pupils were at recess. The school principal, Burton Wragg (fifty-three), was standing at the gate. With her first shot Brenda hit him in the neck and he died instantly. Pupils Paul Carr (eleven) and Jimmy Lira (ten) were hit in the arms and legs. The custodian, Michael Sucher (fifty-six), ran out to help the children on the playground. He was fatally wounded by a bullet to the head. The girl at the window went on shooting. . . . Mr. Bill Kolander, San Diego's chief of police, tried to calm the trigger-happy schoolgirl by telephone. . . . Six hours went by. . . . When she was taken away by the police, she said, 'I didn't have any idea how this thing worked. . . . When they all fell to the ground, I thought it was fun, and I kept on shooting.' "

New York Post, November 1, 1979: "Forty youths beat

and stabbed a motorist. A couple walking on Rockaway Boulevard was told to trick or treat and then the man was shot in the spine and stabbed in the thigh. Two youths wearing Halloween masks doused a subway token stand with gasoline and threatened to burn the clerk inside."

Neue Zürcher Zeitung (Switzerland), September 21, 1981: "Numerous injuries, traffic jams, and shattered windows were the result of a department store's advertisement offering free admission on Saturday to movie theaters in Berne and Biel in celebration of the store's hundredth anniversary. Thousands tried to take advantage of the offer. The police officer in charge in Biel said: 'It was a revolting sight the way several hundred people pushed their way like animals into a movie theater in which two hundred fifty people had already taken every available space. Those weren't human beings anymore.' "

New York Post, February 28, 1984: "Eleven Westchester men heading home after a night on the town ripped apart a four-car commuter train and terrified 250 passengers aboard. Most of the men were in their early 20's."

Zuger Tageblatt, October 12, 1979: "An irate gym teacher from Ticino was sentenced to one and a half years in prison for breaking in two places the arm of one of his pupils with a powerful kick and several blows. . . . On March 16 of this year he ordered his class to run a race around the gym in a crouching position as a disciplinary action. Fourteen-year-old Tiziano Consoli wasn't able to do this at the required speed and had to repeat it with the fastest sprinter in the class. Physically somewhat frail, he dropped out of the race. Amid the laughter of Tiziano's schoolmates, the teacher, known for his militaristic methods of keeping order, kicked and repeatedly hit the helpless boy with full force."

Tages-Anzeiger (Switzerland), September 3, 1985: "On Monday in Piraeus near Athens legal proceedings were initiated against the captain and ten crew members of the Greek freighter *Garifalia*. They are accused of throwing overboard eleven blind passengers from Kenya last year and leaving them to their fate in shark-infested waters. According to the findings of the Greek authorities, apparently none of the victims survived."

Tages-Anzeiger, September 24, 1985: "An approximately twenty-year-old archer played a dangerous 'joke' on Sunday morning . . . ; shortly after 11 A.M. the unidentified archer shot an arrow from the bank of the Rhine River at a passenger on a boat, seriously injuring him."

Boston Globe, February 26, 1986: "Three young Quincy men admitted beating and kicking to death a Vietnam War veteran turned homeless alcoholic after stealing his whiskey and his last $4 as he lay sleeping in the vestibule of a Quincy apartment building."

Tages-Anzeiger, June 21, 1985: "The Japanese press on Thursday, in a rare display of unanimity, criticized the behavior of approximately forty reporters, who on Tuesday evening photographed the murder of suspected swindler Toyota Shoji without trying to stop the murderers. . . . [The reporters] took pictures of the two radical Right murderers as they entered [Shoji's] home through a window and came back out covered with blood. [Instead of intervening] the reporters fought with one another for the best spots from which to film."

IN *CRIMINAL VIOLENCE, Criminal Justice* (1978), Charles E. Silberman documents not only an increase in violent crime in the United States but also the growing number of youthful offenders. In 1967, 44 percent of those arrested for rape and over 26 percent of those arrested for assault and homicide were between the ages of eighteen and twenty-four. Fifty percent of those apprehended for burglary and larceny were under eighteen. Moreover, there seems to be a connection between the youth of the offenders and the unusual viciousness of their crimes. Silberman notes that the frequent maim-

ing or killing of victims was not essential to carrying out
many of these crimes but must have stemmed from underlying rage and brutality. He also points out that poverty is not
a decisive factor in criminality. For example, the crime rate
among the low-income Hispanic population is significantly
lower than that among low-income blacks.[60]

These findings, along with the fact that there was little
crime in Portugal during Antonio Salazar's dictatorship,
point to two prerequisites for soaring criminal violence. The
first: subliminal hatred generated by the compulsion to conform. The second: when the authority structure collapses
and the promises that have made people submit to power
and sacrifice their feelings of self-esteem are no longer kept,
hatred erupts; as long as authority maintains its grip, people
are deterred from open violence.

Japan, a country with a strongly conformist social structure, is experiencing an upsurge in brutality in its schools.
There are more and more reports of suicide by pupils who
can no longer bear the harassment at school. The recorded
cases of violent acts in the schools increased 23 percent in
1985 alone. Bands of pupils sadistically tortured their
weaker classmates.[61]

Hiroshi Kusunokie, a teacher in Japan, asked his pupils
to write an essay about what they would do if they had only
five more days to live. An eleven-year-old wrote: "The first
day I would eat especially well. On the second day I would
go to a casino and gamble away a lot of money. On the
third day I would get myself a pistol, on the fourth go on a
world tour and go swimming on Waikiki Beach in Hawaii.
On the day I'm going to die I'll beat up my father, trample
on him, and at eleven o'clock fifty-nine minutes and fifty-
nine seconds I'll jump on the train for heaven." A twelve-
year-old wrote that on the first day he would smash all the
windows, then rob a bank and burn all the money, then
dismember a human body the way he had often seen it done
on television, set fire to a house, run down more than three
hundred people with a car, and "when I've done all that, I

won't mind dying." In other essays, the children described throwing bombs, dismembering their parents, and so on.[62] The essential thing for these children seems to be destructiveness for its own sake.

Quite a bit earlier than these examples from Japan, in 1972 an English schoolteacher, Muriel Hirsch, wrote about her class:

> "I hate school!" said Ron on my first day in my new job.
> . . . "[E]veryone does. Let's face it—I hate the teachers and the teachers hate me. *You* hate me. . . ."
> "Well—no. Not yet. I don't really know you well enough to hate you."
> "Well . . ." he accepted the point grudgingly. . . .
> It was real deep hatred he was talking about, engendered in a life-long battle.[63]

His kind of insolence, Hirsch continues, is very hard for teachers to take, so that the hatred soon becomes mutual and the authorities no longer know how to deal with it.

> Such boys appear to be totally apathetic about politics. "Who knows the meaning of the word 'communism?' "—"No one, miss."—"Oh miss, can't we do something interesting. . . ." The only thing they'll admit to being interested in is sex. Yet they have IRA written all over their books and satchels. "Who can tell me about the IRA? What is the conflict about in Northern Ireland?"
> "Oh, the Catholics hate the Protestants—can't we do something interestin'?"
> "If you're not interested, why do you support the IRA?"
> "Cor—because they throw bombs and smash things— blow people up—gr . . . reat!"[64]

Referring to her pupils' attitudes, Hirsch says:

> Perhaps the children in Belfast feel the same. It's the violence they like—not the human rights. It's their parents and teachers they hate—not the Protestants.

All their lives violence has been the pattern. "Do you know," says the beautifully groomed young mum, waiting outside the infants' school, "she cried every morning last week at having to go to school . . . I gave her a good hiding—in fact she's had several—but she's no better!" Violence at home, violence at school. One of the earliest lessons to be driven home to them all. Being forced to go to a place you hate and fear. No wonder they refuse to learn to read and write. . . .[65]

Hirsch then describes how the supposedly "lax" style of teaching, insofar as it exists at all, applies only to the bright, conformist pupils, whereas the others are dealt with harshly. The headmasters are increasingly autocratic, and liberal teachers, who do not want simply to exercise iron discipline, scarcely have a chance. Consequently, the school itself has created the situation that it claims justifies its procedures.

Hirsch sees a vicious circle here: children who are habitually punished at home and behave badly at school actually seek punishment, because they do not understand and cannot accept friendliness and kindness. Perhaps there is an advantage to this. Children who reject friendliness and refuse to be dependent at least have no illusions and do not subscribe to the usual hypocrisy. But the result is what I call violence or rebellion "without ideology." Destructiveness becomes a way of life. At the same time, this destructiveness is a cry for help. But since the conformist attitude knows only punishment, it responds not to the cry for help but to rebelliousness—and in a totally inappropriate manner that leads only to an increase in blind and destructive rage.

Sadism and Rebellion

Torture carried out by the state and the terrorist's attack are extreme manifestations of conformity and rebellion respectively. Conformist sadists are usually people with official power—or, like the members of the Latin American death squads, those who receive protection from the government—who must silence their victims in order to blot out the memory of their own submission. Terrorists have no official power; their revenge is directed against the power of the oppressors, from whom they secretly want recognition.

One of the most eloquent witnesses to the sadist's behavior is Jacobo Timerman. Describing his own torture under the Argentinian junta and its army of sadists in *Prisoner without a Name, Cell without a Number*, he emphasizes that their aim was not repression but total eradication. From this we can deduce that their own submission to authority must have been extreme and, therefore, accompanied by ferocious self-hatred. In a conversation Timerman had with an Argentinian naval officer, the officer said: "[I]f we exterminate them all [the subversives], there'll be fear for several generations. . . . And their relatives, too—they must be eradicated—and also those who remember their names."[66] These words, of course, reveal the panic sadists feel because there might be a witness who could tell about their shameful deeds and their weakness, about their abject fusion with authority in order to escape their vulnerability. They hate everything that reminds them of humaneness. "The chief obsession of the totalitarian mind lies in its need for the world to be clearcut and orderly. Any subtlety, contradiction, or complexity upsets and confuses this notion and becomes intolerable. Whereupon an attempt is made to overcome the intolerable by way of the only method at hand—violence."[67]

The Nigerian writer Wole Soyinka, winner of the Nobel Prize in Literature in 1986, who was imprisoned in Nigeria for his independent thinking, describes his torturers by quoting them: " 'But what gives people like you . . . the right to think that you know everything? . . . When the government has already laid down a policy, what makes you think you know better? You are intellectuals living in a dream world, yet you think you know better than men who have weighed out so many factors and come to a decision.' " And: " 'We have re-created truth and truth is now defined in our image. . . . Truth, my dear friend, is the thousands who have vanished since we fixed your interfering little mind!' "[68]

Soyinka knows that by torturing, the sadist re-creates the terror of his early childhood. His victim is supposed to feel the presence of a merciless God who promises salvation in return for submitting to him and for acknowledging his goodness; Soyinka describes the prisoner's desire to surrender and to place his soul entirely into the "loving" hands of the torturer (Timerman, too, repeatedly documents the bond between torturer and victim). The Nigerian writer also knows what the prisoner's antidote for this is: "[T]he prisoner suddenly says to himself, This creature cannot really touch me. He cannot save me therefore he cannot destroy me. This creature is irrelevant, he is not real. I represent reality."[69] Here we see the emergence of a deeply ingrained fantasy latent in all of us: ultimately to be saved by the bad mother. If we renounce this hope—or at least acknowledge it—we can renounce the conformist as well as the rebel in us and begin to find the way to the real self. (I do not mean by "rebel" the revolutionary who, in Erich Fromm's sense, has overcome his bond to authority and the accompanying wish to dominate others.)

Both the conformist and the rebel need an external enemy. This need often makes it impossible to distinguish between real and hallucinated threats. Since 1917, the West has feared the spread of the Red revolution, but actually, after the First World War, the Western democracies were threatened by fascism, not by communism. This was denied, however, until it was almost too late. Similarly, despite the testimony of escapees from the death camps,[70] Polish Jews did not believe that the National Socialists were their greatest enemies. They felt threatened by those who warned them and therefore did not believe the warnings. The need for an enemy comes from inner depths that have nothing to do with outer reality and creates images that both rebel and conform-ist use to justify the worst atrocities.

Conformity is compatible with any ideology; it can be found wherever there is power. Neither the conformist nor the rebel knows the reality of a lived life. Having never loved a real self, each knows nothing of either life or death. Both consider themselves immortal. Their grandiosity nourishes the illusion of a suprahistorical eternity. Both believe they will live on in the monuments they have raised to themselves. For the conformists, these are the monuments of stone and concrete erected by the powerful people they serve; for the rebels, they are their own "grandiose" deeds.

It is those who have never accepted life's realities who always think there is an escape. That is why, for example, many people believe in building bomb shelters. It does not occur to them that life might not be worth living if the conditions for a life worthy of human beings no longer exist.

The conformist and the rebel need each other; both need the violence of the other to validate their image of the enemy. The rebel, however, at least keeps alive our awareness of the possibilities for change and the hope kindled in all of us by our experience of the good mother. If we could succeed in bringing rebels into closer contact with their pain, then they might not have the compulsion to play the role of the enemy, which conformists need to keep from going insane.

V I

Power Politics as an Expression of Inner Emptiness

NO MATTER HOW much lip service those committed to power may pay to the principle of equality, they can never approach their fellow human beings on an equal footing; their relationships with others are defined solely in terms of power or weakness. Therefore, they must accumulate as much power as possible with the aim of becoming invulnerable and proving this invulnerability.

One of the most horrible results of such a distorted approach to reality was the war between the United States and North Vietnam. In their struggle to achieve military goals, the North Vietnamese government also took into account the morale of their people, as well as that of their opponents. They did not see victory and success solely from the perspective of a narrow notion of strength. The American policy makers, however, were guided by a conception of strength based on childhood experiences of being overwhelmed by parental power. From this, they drew the lesson that causing pain is the way to control people. Consequently, anything other than a politics of power and superior strength is unimaginable.

It was this kind of thinking that determined Richard Nixon's approach to the Vietnam conflict during his administration. Nixon was a man for whom nothing but power mattered. Every one of his actions throughout his political career was characterized by contempt for humanity. His own words betray that for him inflicting pain on others was the only way to influence their behavior.

This attitude led Nixon to conduct the most barbarous bombing raids of the Vietnam War, thus revealing his utter disregard for human life. He explained his method of reasoning in his book *No More Vietnams*. A week before Christmas 1972, he ordered heavy air attacks on the Hanoi-Haiphong corridor to show the North Vietnamese that they would not be able to violate the peace accord, almost reached, with impunity.[1] For eleven days U.S. planes conducted the most concentrated air offensive of the war against North Vietnam, not for the sake of military advantage but simply to impress the enemy with America's superior force. The extent of Nixon's obsession with demonstrating his power—or with, as he called it, "real politics"—has a very personal origin, as can be seen from his remarks to the chairman of the Joint Chiefs of Staff: "I don't want any more of this crap about the fact that we couldn't hit this target or that one. This is your chance to use military power to win this war, and if you don't, I'll hold you responsible."[2]

This kind of "signaling," with which we are familiar from the Second World War, is not based on a realistic assessment of the enemy's ability to hold out but is the expression of a purely personal delusion, which in the case of the air attack mentioned above resulted in 1,623 civilian deaths among the Vietnamese and in heavy American casualties. Previously, in May 1972, Nixon, the first U.S. president to visit the Soviet Union, sent another signal on the eve of his scheduled summit meeting in Moscow with Soviet Premier Leonid Brezhnev by ordering the bombing of Hanoi and the mining of Haiphong Harbor. The reason he gave was to halt a North Vietnamese offensive in the south, but he later revealed that his strategy had to do with power politics: "But I believed that if we allowed North Vietnam to conquer South Vietnam," he writes, "the hardheaded realists in the politburos in Peking and Moscow might think a United States that lacked the will to defend its interest was not worth talking to." What would better show American decisiveness and strength than the willingness to demolish Moscow's ally North Vietnam? And Nixon continues: "[Brezhnev] knew we were worth talking to, because our actions in Vietnam had demonstrated that we had not only the power to defend our interests but also the will to use it. If we had not acted . . . [w]e would have been in an intolerable position of weakness. Brezhnev would have assumed that if I could be pushed around in Vietnam, I could also be pushed around in Moscow."[3] This is how power dictates what "reality" is and brutally enforces it. The only reality here is the mythology of power based on a little boy's fantasy of ruthless domination. Such little boys entertain these fantasies because their earliest experience is one of submission to the power of their parents.

The interior world of these power-obsessed men is filled with both self-hatred and emptiness. In his memoirs, Henry Kissinger describes how Nixon greeted his White House staff and cabinet the morning after his overwhelming election victory in November 1972 by demanding their resignations. This illogical reaction prompted Kissinger to observe: "It was almost as if [his victory at the polls] had been sought for its own sake; as if, standing on the pinnacle, Nixon no longer had any purpose left to his life. . . . Triumph seemed to fill Nixon with a premonition of ephemerality. He was, as he never tired of repeating, at his best under pressure. Indeed, it was sometimes difficult to avoid the impression that he needed crises as a motivating force—and that success became not a goal but an obsession so that once achieved he would not know what to do with it."[4]

In a review of Nixon and his times, Ronald Steel writes about Nixon's life and, in particular, about his handling of the Watergate affair: "He threw his prize [the presidency] away as if, in some unconscious way, he sought to render valueless what he had won at such cost. Whether he did so because in the depths of his heart he felt he was unworthy, and thus had to diminish not only the meaning of the prize but the prize itself, or whether it was from some irresistible compulsion forever to create new crises to be measured against and struggle to surmount—none of this will we ever know."[5] But we can know if we are willing to see that both self-contempt and the lust for power have the same roots—namely, in the loss of autonomy.

When a boy becomes an adult like Nixon, full of ambition—empty as it may be—he will continue to try to live up to the expectations of a mother who substituted her will for his. And in the actions of such men, there always lurks a flirtation with death and danger, a playing with the lives of other people; by risking failure and causing the whole ambitious structure around them to collapse, they are taking revenge on their mother: they are deliberately negating what she tried to achieve through them.

The only way to end the Vietnam War, Nixon writes, was to get things moving on the negotiating front by taking action on the military front.[6] He and his secretary of state, Henry Kissinger, were therefore fixated on "decisiveness" and "fire-power" as the only dimensions of their reality, and it was in this spirit that they conducted foreign policy. How unrealistic this position was, especially during the Vietnam War, is succinctly elucidated by an exchange during the final peace negotiations: Col. Harry G. Summers reports that an American negotiator said to his North Vietnamese counterpart, "You know you never defeated us on the battlefield." "That may be so," the latter replied, "but it is also irrelevant."[7]

The view of reality of the North Vietnamese encompassed more aspects of human life than power alone. To them, for instance, pain and suffering were not primarily means to intimidate others. (This is not to say that the North Vietnamese were not cruel, that they did not torture American prisoners. In any social grouping, there are always people who think they can dominate others by inflicting pain; what is crucial is whether they are in control of national policy or not.) The North Vietnamese understood, on the contrary, that pain and suffering can strengthen people's resolve *not* to surrender. This insight was inaccessible to the American "realists," for their notion of reality was formed by the experience of power they had had in childhood. As children, they had taken refuge from pain and humiliation in conformity, and, therefore, as adults they could no longer imagine other ways of reacting.

The history of humankind is rich in examples of the effects of a diminished perception of reality. Barbara Tuchman tellingly entitled her study of wars from Troy to Vietnam *The March of Folly.* "Folly," she writes, "is a child of power. We all know . . . that power corrupts. We are less aware that it breeds folly; that the power to command frequently causes failure to think. . . ."[8] I would say it is not so much failure to think that plays a role here as it is a *reduction* in thinking. And this reduction, in turn, is a result of emotional processes directly connected to the thinker's early conformity to power and flight from pain. People like Nixon, who see the world simply as an input-output mechanism in which pain or its anticipation is the lever for controlling other people, demonstrate by their actions their own failure to come to terms with pain by any means other than abject surrender.

This surrender has as its ultimate goal the appropriation of the power one submitted to, and it is always part of an unverbalized proposal: "I will yield to you in order to partake of your power." With this tacit aim, people conceal the self-hatred they feel for having submitted. They will then be unable to acknowledge any reality not defined in terms of power. Their quest for power becomes compulsive, and their inability to tolerate pain, which they have come to equate with humiliation, makes them avoid it at all cost. Yet they will not avoid inflicting pain on other people; indeed, humiliating and degrading others becomes their central purpose in life.

This attitude of course requires the existence of an enemy

to furnish justification for one's need for power and for the conquests motivated by self-hatred. What needs to be conquered can be a mountain peak, a scientific problem, a nature preserve standing in the way of a highway, or a flesh-and-blood enemy. The need is for an enemy or a "challenge." Since most of us are similar in this respect, we are prone to seek relief from inner doubts and feelings of hatred in this way. We are all too easily induced to feel threatened by external enemies. The degree to which we require such enemies to relieve our inner disquiet determines in the last analysis how willing we are to follow a leader who offers us a suitable enemy.

Even seemingly "sane" leaders are not immune to this view of reality. In his autobiography, the German psychoanalyst Horst Eberhard Richter describes a meeting with the former German chancellor Helmut Schmidt, a Social Democrat, who criticized Richter for calling the sensitive, open, and vulnerable personality richer and healthier than the robust one that can adapt to anything.[9] All representatives of the ideology of power, which is based on a false conception of the self, fear people who are inner-directed and have contempt for them because it is a fear that cannot be acknowledged. It makes no difference whether one is on the Left or Right politically. What we are faced with on all sides is an obsession with power, rather than an openness to reality with all its rich and vital possibilities.

This becomes a problem for all of us because it is the power obsessed who are in positions from which they can determine our history. Those in high places, with their fixation on power and their compulsive need to attain it, often exhibit the greatest inner emptiness. Barbara Tuchman develops this theme in her book, giving examples of how the powerful reduce reality. During the American Revolution, when the British army under the command of General Burgoyne surrendered to the Continental army at Saratoga on October 17, 1777, the English government and people were stunned.[10] Yet the English government survived all the attacks made on it in Parliament because no one wanted to face the fact that the surrender came as a result of an inadequate concept of reality; for then it would have become clear that the "realism" of the power politicians was devoid of all awareness of actual human reality.

Using the example of the British reaction to the capture and burning of the British customs schooner *Gaspée* by Rhode Island colonists in 1772, Tuchman shows how those who insist most on the "realism" of power politics also feel the most justified in exercising power ruthlessly. The two legal officers of the Crown, who declared this protest against English imperialism an act of treason against the king and wanted to bring the culprits to trial in England, were Edward Thurlow, attorney-general, and Alexander Wedderburn, solicitor-general. Both personified men who compensate for their inner emptiness by means of external aggrandizement. "Unmanageable as a schoolboy . . . surly and assertive in the law, Thurlow had a savage temper and reputedly the foulest mouth in London. He was nevertheless an impressive figure. . . . [T]he King eventually rewarded his firm support with appointment as Lord Chancellor and a barony to go with it. Equally coercive as regards America, Wedderburn was a Scot of voracious ambition who would use any means . . . to gain advancement. . . . Although despised by the King, he too eventually became Lord Chancellor."[11]

Obviously, men of this type are adaptable, and their "realism" fluctuates according to the specific events and needs of their time. Two hundred years after the American Revolution, the approach to warfare was of course changing. The military concept of massive retaliation, for instance, which had been the dominant doctrine under the Eisenhower administration, underwent a major modification when John F. Kennedy took office in 1961. The new president surrounded himself with men who were bright, realistic, sophisticated, pragmatic, and tough. His secretary of defense, Robert

McNamara, was a specialist in "statistical analysis" who had boundless confidence that for every problem there was a solution and who believed in the effectiveness of military matériel. The policy of massive retaliation was changed under Kennedy and McNamara to one of "limited war." "Its aim was not conquest but coercion; force would be used on a rationally calculated basis to alter the enemy's will and capabilities to the point where 'the advantages of terminating the conflict were greater than the advantages of continuing it.' "[12]

The formulas change, to be sure, but their essence remains the same: namely, "to alter the enemy's will and capabilities." With the new game plan for war, the "new" men made war into something that could be "managed . . . in such a way as to send messages to the opposing belligerent, who would respond rationally to the pain and damage inflicted on him by desisting from the actions that cause them."[13] This kind of rational management conceals the madness of believing human beings can be coerced by having pain inflicted on them. "We are flung into a straitjacket of rationality," said William Kaufman, one of the new ideologues of U.S. power, as quoted by Tuchman.

This attitude does not, however, take into account that there are people who deal differently with pain and do not submit because of it. The "realistic" type, who thinks reality is solely a question of capitulating to a superior force, knows nothing of the strength of those who, despite suffering, do not cease listening to their inner self. Perhaps that is why U.S. intervention in Vietnam was a lost cause.

Again and again, as Tuchman so vividly illustrates, history is a record of the actions of "realists" who keep leading us to destruction. She gives another example: during the Berlin crisis in the summer of 1961, Kennedy said to a journalist after a difficult meeting with Khrushchev in Vienna, "Now we have a problem in making our power credible, and Vietnam looks like the place."[14] Because Khrushchev did not react appropriately to Kennedy as the representative of a great power, proof of this had to be provided. The value of human life did not appear to be given any consideration when it was a matter of making power "credible," nor did the fact that the Vietnamese people were struggling to achieve self-determination have any meaning for the U.S. proponents of realpolitik. That escalating the war also meant perverting the struggle for self-determination is another story. When such a struggle is thwarted, the "realists" among the revolutionaries, too, gain the upper hand because their shortsightedness promises quicker success. In the end, the two sides will be much more alike than in the beginning.

President Kennedy also demonstrated how a political leader, a captive of his own power role, forsakes whatever real feelings are still accessible to him. Sen. Mike Mansfield, after returning from an inspection tour in South Vietnam made at the president's request, warned him against deeper involvement there:

> The infusion of American troops would come to dominate a civil war that was not our affair. Taking it over would "hurt American prestige in Asia and would not help the South Vietnamese to stand on their own feet either." Growing more disturbed and red in the face as Mansfield talked, Kennedy snapped at him, "Do you expect me to take this at face value?" Like all rulers, he wanted to be confirmed in his policy and was angry at Mansfield, as he confessed to an aide later, for disagreeing so completely, "and angry at myself because I found myself agreeing with him."[15]

What made Kennedy continue with a policy he himself considered wrong? Essentially, it was a lack of feeling for the suffering he would be inflicting on human beings. He was anxious to win a second term. Several months later, he assured Mansfield that he was leaning more and more toward military withdrawal from Vietnam. "But I can't do it until 1965—until after I'm reelected."[16] Power meant more to him than human life.

How different a man was Abraham Lincoln, a leader who never tried to avoid his inner life. He is a prime example for

me that power need not corrupt, provided that the preconditions for corruption are not present in a person. Lincoln had
a great capacity for experiencing joy and sorrow. His sense
of responsibility stemmed from this capacity. He knew that
the pain of the human condition could not be numbed with
palliatives. He was aware that it was something that had to
be accepted, that it was deep within us and inaccessible to
any kind of easy manipulation. Lincoln's sense of humor was
based on his ability to laugh at himself, as Carl Sandburg
frequently documents in his biography.[17] People who are
caught up in self-hatred do not have this ability. A man like
Lincoln was able to ease his pain with humor instead of
running away from it by means of self-aggrandizement.

Lincoln commuted the death sentence of deserters whenever possible. "No one need ever expect me to sanction the
shooting of a man for running away in battle, I won't do it. A
man can't help being a coward any more than he could help
being a humpback."[18] He valued life for its own sake, without worrying about his own political image. "You cannot
order men shot by dozens or twenties. People . . . ought not
to stand it. No, we must change the condition of things some
other way."[19] He defined very clearly a human being's true
responsibility: "I desire to so conduct the affairs of this
administration that if, at the end, when I come to lay down
the reins of power, I have lost every other friend on earth, I
shall at least have one friend left, and that friend shall be
down inside of me."[20]

For the people Tuchman describes, the issue is not simply a
lust for power. That is only the symptom of a genuine mental
illness originating in the loss of autonomy. Those afflicted
are wholly outer-directed and are always concerned with
appearing in a favorable light; therefore, their insanity has
not been recognized for what it is: the denial of reality in the
name of realism. These "realists" are not deficient in intellectual prowess, but they cannot give it free rein because they
must maintain the Basic Lie at any cost and make a lifelong

attempt to deny the inner self the right to exist. This is why, one way or another, they will always be intent on silencing the inner voice in themselves and others. They resemble George Orwell's Grand Inquisitor in *1984*, who cannot tolerate the inner doubts of his victims. Their actions are less of a problem for him; it is the inner self that he must kill in them as well as in himself.

This undiagnosed insanity is more of a threat to humankind today than ever before because the means of destruction in the hands of the power hungry have never been greater. Illness of this kind differs from schizophrenia in one crucial aspect: schizophrenics struggle with themselves in an effort to come to terms with an intolerable world, whereas the power hungry, who are considered sane, struggle to subdue other people in order to feel secure themselves.

Apart from its literary merits, Umberto Eco's novel *The Name of the Rose* is a study of male insanity in its countless everyday aspects. As in the world we know, here, too, insane actions are carried out in the name of "realism." Through William, a monk who travels on diplomatic missions, we are given a glimpse of the motives behind men's quest for power: to overcome their fear of death, they all set themselves the goal of attaining power. Eco shows how various are the means by which they attempt to reach this goal, and this is what gives the book its great breadth and subtlety. No one, with the exception of the one woman in the novel, a pretty peasant girl with a hunger for life, resists the temptations of power. Although all the other characters proclaim their willingness to suffer as God's servants on earth, they evade the implications of this role. Eco presents the countless ways of building a power base, but they all have the same goal: to avoid suffering.

For Bernard Gui, the inquisitor, the use of naked power is the way to win control of people's souls. For Jorge of Burgos, the librarian, it is the possession of a book that contains a threat to existing authority. He murders anyone who tries to gain possession of it, for the book can be seen as a symbol of the rejected self, as the source of true freedom. The world-wide fascination with this novel must lie in the way it holds a mirror up to male insanity, even though most of its readers might not be conscious of this. It is as though they do sense and experience something of this insanity, only to put the book down with the feeling that they have participated vicariously in a horrifying but exciting reality.

In his portrait of the inquisitor, Eco describes the nature of a man for whom power over others is everything. Such men are not concerned with justice when they persecute and prosecute dissidents, not even within the framework of their own ideology; they are merely searching for sacrificial victims in order to maintain the appearance of justice. Thus, they are not interested in the actual culprit; like Bernard Gui in the novel, they simply need someone, anyone, whom they can condemn and punish. What matters is the discharge of aggression and revenge, not finding the actual guilty person. The legal history of every society, but especially of totalitarian ones, is filled with this kind of perversion. Bernard even prevents William from finding the real murderer in the abbey.

The persecution of others is only one of the moves in a larger power game. Eco has an intuitive understanding of how the power hungry bring their victims around to collaborating with them. In previous chapters, I have explained how it comes about that victims submit, how children are motivated to surrender by the parental promise that they will be taken care of, and how they are rewarded for their surrender by being absolved of taking responsibility for themselves.

Eco shows that he understands this phenomenon by having Bernard Gui take advantage of his victims' past history of collaboration in their submission: they fear him and, at the same time, hope that he will mercifully forgive them the trespasses of which he has accused them: "Gui, for his part, knew how to transform his victims' fear into terror. He did not speak. . . . His gaze was really fixed on the accused, and it was a gaze in which hypocritical indulgence (as if to say: Never fear, you are in the hands of a fraternal assembly that can only want your good) mixed with icy irony (as if to say: You do not yet know what your good is, and I will shortly tell you) and merciless severity (as if to say: But in any case I am your judge here, and you are in my power)."[21] Here, Eco lets us experience terror and emotional seduction that are very similar to what children undergo; he shows how the victims again succumb to this seduction, becoming the tools of their torturers just as they once were the tools of their parents. The fantasy of being saved by the bad mother or the bad father lives on, a form of dependency that becomes a curse because it prevents one from realizing one can save oneself only by finding the true self.

Eco also knows that fear is at the heart of self-enslavement and that the ability to laugh at oneself robs it of its power. For this reason, the character Jorge feels compelled to destroy the book in the name of Christ, for it speaks of laughter, and laughter might dispel the fear of fear. Jorge wants to retain the use of fear as a powerful weapon to keep people enslaved. No one may read the forbidden book, the second part of Aristotle's *Poetics*—which, according to Eco's novel, did exist until it went up in flames with the rest of the abbey—because it deals with comedy and laughter and, therefore, points the way out of the vicious circle of enslavement. Jorge's insanity and the malevolence with which he pursues his goal are of course concealed under the cloak of piety.

It may seem a far cry from the characters in *The Name of the Rose* to former President Reagan, but he, too, is a leader for whom the conquest of the external world serves as a flight from the inner self. This makes him similar in certain ways to the characters in Eco's novel. Reagan not only illustrates the bond between such a leader and a public desperately seeking release from a self it cannot tolerate, but also documents this type of dissociation himself in an autobiography appropriately titled *Where's the Rest of Me?*

In a brilliant and provocative book, *Ronald Reagan, the Movie and Other Episodes in Political Demonology*, Michael Rogin concludes that Reagan knew who he was only when playing a role in a film. Rogin's characterization of Reagan supports the thesis that in an attempt to escape his inner self, he is wholly outer-directed. Rogin believes that by confusing movies and life, Reagan became the man he did, which of course makes him appear to be a product of circumstances over which he had no control.[22] Here I must take issue, for the life of people like Reagan is marked by the deliberate attempt to arrange things so that they do not have to face the inner self. If we see Reagan only as a victim of circumstances, we will not notice that it is the rejection of personal responsibility that characterizes such leaders, and we will excuse the evil inherent in their actions.

To be sure, psychological and sociological determinants do play a certain role, but I have repeatedly attempted to show that there is an element of choice in the way human beings develop. If we do not keep this in mind, we will overlook the hatred and contempt that motivate people like Reagan. To "understand" them makes us all too prone to pity them, but pity only serves to make us feel superior to those who harm us, so that we end up denying their hatred and their contempt.

Rogin gives an example that shows Reagan is not simply cut off from himself: once, when governor of California, he refused to visit a mental hospital affected by his budget cuts. A hospital psychiatrist suggested that Reagan was under strain, to which the governor responded, "If I get on that couch, it will be to take a nap." Rogin thinks this is a sign that Reagan has no unconscious.[23] I submit, however, that it is not only inaccessible to him but that he actively and contemptuously rejects it. He hates the inner life and turns his hatred into mockery if anyone refers to the possible existence of an inner world. By saying he would use it only to take a nap, he makes a joke of the couch, a place meant for inner exploration. Another point to be made is that Reagan's fear of needing help is so great that he must refuse it even when it has not been explicitly offered to him. For having no inner problems is proof to him of independence. If we fail to perceive this vehement rejection of and contempt for the inner world in such people, we will also overlook the constant undercurrent of aggression they harbor.

People like Reagan fear the evil within themselves, even while giving expression to it. That is why they must cut themselves off from their inner self or—as Rogin puts it, referring to a famous scene in one of Reagan's films— acquire an amputated self.[24] Reagan is unable to face his inner turmoil; he therefore projects it outward. This is the deeper meaning of the title *Where's the Rest of Me?* What is really at issue is the process by which he objectifies what he hates and fears within himself, transforming it into an external enemy attacking him from the outside. "Now I had become a semi-automaton 'creating' a character another had written, doing what still another person told me to do on the set. Seeing the rushes, I could barely believe the colored shadow on the screen was myself. Possibly this was the reason I decided to find the rest of me. I loved three things: drama, politics, and sports. . . . In all three of them I came out of the monastery of movies into the world." Fighting the villain in the movie was no longer enough for him; in 1946 he took up the struggle against what he saw as the Communist takeover of the film industry.[25] That is how he found the lost part of himself. He projected outward the danger within his own soul in order to conquer it as a concrete enemy. This was, of course, made easier for him because many people tend to avoid unpleasant inner truths the same way he did. Following this logic, it comes as no surprise that Reagan proudly admitted that as president of the Screen Actors Guild he carried a gun for "protection."[26]

Behind this split between inner and outer, there is hidden in such men not only submission to the mother but also fury, no less hidden, at a father who failed to protect them from the mother's claims to power.

Volker Elis Pilgrim, in his thought-provoking book *Muttersöhne* ("Mothers' Sons"), advances the daring thesis that men like Hitler, Stalin, and Napoleon, who hated other men because they hated their fathers, had essentially feminine traits. Before they turned into murderers, they were "sensitive, delicate, profound, mysterious."[27] Pilgrim is on the right track—all three men had a special relationship with their mothers and were dominated by them—but he makes a serious error by referring to these men as feminine and as "would-be girls." What Pilgrim mistakenly takes for their femininity is nothing other than what all macho thinking considers feminine: the proclivity for self-pity. That is not a feminine trait but is, rather, part and parcel of the fundamental self-deception that submitting to power is not one's own fault. The reason these men submitted to the mother was to partake of her power. Their ensuing self-pity—"I couldn't help it!"—did not come from genuine feelings but from the need to avoid them. What Pilgrim thinks of as sensitivity is counterfeit. These "sensitive" men merely felt sorry for themselves and wanted to make the world share in their self-deception. Their so-called feminine qualities are a mockery of true femininity; it is a femininity seen through the eyes of the patriarchy that distorts female attributes in order to disparage them.

Pilgrim cites reports according to which Hitler is supposed to have had a tendency to cry and sees in this, among other things, evidence of his femininity.[28] What he does not see is the fact that it is precisely this crying that is intended to awaken pity and direct attention away from one's guilt. It is the kind of crying that children learn to do when they notice that their mothers react with "love" only to "contrition," not to real sadness. That these children, as adult males, scorn feminine qualities should come as no surprise. All the "mothers' sons" Pilgrim describes hated their mothers. If these men had really been feminine, they would have loved their mothers. But that was impossible because every surrender of the self breeds secret hatred, self-hatred as well as hatred for the person to whom one has surrendered.

To a certain extent, Pilgrim recognizes this hatred, yet he fails to notice that it results not in a genuine identification with the mother but in a mockery of the femininity she represents. (And he reminds us that Napoleon and Hitler conducted or planned wars against an ur-symbol of the mother—"Mother Russia."[29]) It is, of course, quite true that these men professed to love their mothers, but their love was not genuine. Eduard Bloch, the physician who treated Hitler's mother in 1907, later commented that he had "never seen a youngster so *ineffably saddened* with grief and sorrow as young Adolf Hitler" at his mother's funeral.[30] Yet what lies behind this sort of hysterical devotion found in many conformists? Pilgrim believes that Hitler's hatred of Jews had something to do with the fact that Dr. Bloch, a Jew, had not been able to help his mother in her struggle against breast cancer.[31] Actually, Hitler showed special consideration for this man, issuing a decree granting him "all possible alleviations, including monetary" after the Anschluss of Austria.[32]

In this regard, Rudolph Binion's analysis is more convincing than Pilgrim's. By drawing on records from Bloch's casebook, which Binion found in the former Central Archives of the Nazi party, he was able to show the split nature of Hitler's "love" for his mother. Although it is true that Hitler tenderly nursed her when she was dying, it was he who insisted on the ineffective but drastic idioform treatment, which caused her great suffering and hastened her death. He was unable to accept the fact that her illness was incurable. Uncertainty was something for which he had no tolerance. "Hitler's experience of his mother's last illness looms behind his later tireless diatribes against the Jewish cancer, the Jewish poison, the Jewish profiteer."[33] Here we have a glimpse of the true nature of Hitler's relationship with his mother, which did not consist of love but of impatience on a conscious level and hatred, probably on an unconscious level. Hatred and an obsession with death are inevitable elements in a relationship in which the child has exchanged autonomy for power. In Hitler's case, his power derived from the importance he had for his mother—even to her death! But it is a power gained only at the expense of one's own truth, and it results in dependency, which is then of course denied.

Michael Rogin sees this quite clearly in the case of Ronald Reagan as well: "Reagan has realized the dream of the American male, to be taken care of in the name of independence, to be supported while playing the man in charge."[34] Reagan's obsession with death is less evident. With Hitler it was unmistakable; with Reagan, however, it simply took another form—namely, an obsessive propensity to think in apocalyptic terms. Neither man admitted to ever having any accompanying fears. That is what is so frightening: a complete lack of fear indicates a high degree of dissociation from real human feelings.

The *Atlanta Journal-Constitution* of October 29, 1983, carried an Associated Press report of what a lobbyist quoted President Reagan as saying to him: " 'You know, I turn back to your ancient prophets in the Old Testament and the signs foretelling Armageddon, and I find myself wondering if—if we're the generation that is going to see that come about. . . . I don't know if you've noted any of those prophesies lately, but, believe me, they certainly describe the times we're going through.' " In Revelation, the last book of the New Testament, Armageddon is prophesied to be the site where demonic powers will gather "the kings of the earth and of the whole world" for the final battle before the Last Judgment. George W. Ball has pointed out that Reagan believed the Soviet Union represented the demonic powers at Armageddon, and therefore *he* did not need to fear this final battle. Considering himself one of the elect, he seemed confident of reigning forever in heaven, while those not chosen are doomed to burn in the eternal fires of the Apocalypse.[35]

The disquieting aspect of these erraticisms is that they reveal how detached a person can be from human feelings. This kind of obsession with death is not accompanied by fear; fear appears only in connection with fantasies concerning national strength. Fear is something that must be instilled in the enemy, with the result that a serious foreign policy is replaced by a buildup of military strength,[36] which forces the enemy to use military strength as a counterthreat. Thus, what has been dissociated in an individual returns in ways that threaten the entire world.

An unexpected witness, Libyan dictator Muammar el-Qaddafi, himself an expert on the subject of death, gave an interview, published in the Italian newspaper *La Repubblica* of April 28, 1986, in which he said of Reagan: "He has grown old, and he has cancer. He wants the world to stop the moment his own life ends. Why should the world still exist after he is gone?" Of course, this also says something about el-Qaddafi, but above all it shows how little importance the lives of other people hold for such men, who harbor the unspoken notion that death is "life." Their preoccupation with death gives them the feeling of being alive.

To return to the theme of the relationship these men had with their mothers: Their surrender to their mothers' demands seems to have been brought about by the unconditional way in which the mother made her son her sole love object. This kind of mother nourishes her son's ambition and grandiosity, which makes him different from ordinary conformists, who do not seek power themselves but are content to join a powerful group. For a son to have his mother's seemingly undivided attention, to feel that he is important to her and that he increases her self-esteem, not only intensifies oedipal feelings vis-à-vis the father but also makes for a secret triumph. This very often takes the form of a subliminal contempt for the father that mirrors the mother's unacknowledged negative feelings toward him.

In his memoirs, former President Nixon provides ample illustration of the special relationship these extremely ambitious men have with their mothers (and fathers): "My father had an Irish quickness both to anger and to mirth. . . . He was a strict and stern disciplinarian, and I tried to follow my mother's example of not crossing him when he was in a bad mood. . . . Everyone who ever knew my mother was impressed with what a remarkable woman she was. . . . Although she radiated warmth and love for her family, indeed, for all people, she was intensely private in her feelings and emotions. . . . Often when I had a difficult decision to make or a speech to prepare, or when I was under attack in the press, my mother would say, 'I will be thinking of you.' "37

Even when his mother nearly caused him serious injury, he did not want to admit it. He describes the incident as follows: "My first conscious memory is of running. I was three years old, and my mother was driving us in a horse-drawn buggy, holding my baby brother Don on her lap while a neighbor girl held me. The horse turned the corner leading to our house at high speed, and I tumbled onto the ground. I must have been in shock, but I managed to get up and run after the buggy while my mother tried to make the horse stop."38 It did not occur to him that his mother was responsible for the accident. This incident as described by Nixon may seem harmless at first glance, and one is inclined to regard it as insignificant. What interests me about it, however, is why Nixon's mother went around a corner at too high a speed. Whatever may have transpired in her conscious mind, she was obviously flirting with danger, which is nothing other than an expression of the destructive feelings hidden in many people.

One consequence of a mother-child relationship in which the child is made to feel that he or she has excessive importance for the mother is an absence of guilt feelings. Whatever the son or daughter does is never wrong in the mother's eyes. As a result, the child develops not only unrestrained delusions of grandeur but also an intensified sense of inner emptiness. For grandiosity diminishes awareness of other people's welfare and, consequently, of their pain and joy. Without this empathy, no inner life can exist. When children feel contempt and hatred for themselves for allowing themselves to be manipulated, they will also feel contempt for the mother who valued them for what they themselves perceive deep within as emptiness.

This emptiness is very concrete. Hitler, for example, is quoted as saying in 1930, when the public was expressing more and more interest in his background, "These people must not learn who I am."[39] And those who, like Reinhold Hanisch, had witnessed the emptiness of his life during the dark days he spent in Viennese shelters for homeless men before the First World War, he had murdered after his annexation of Austria in 1937.[40]

Obviously, not all men in positions of power have mothers who possessed them or fathers who were unavailable. Abraham Lincoln, Franklin D. Roosevelt, and Walter Rathenau, for example, had a very differentiated relationship with their mothers and experienced them as real human beings. Rathenau, Germany's foreign minister during the Weimar Republic, suffered from any limitation on his independence and fought against it with all the means at his disposal. Count Harry Kessler, in his biography of Rathenau, relates a relevant anecdote: Rathenau's mother visited his school to attend his oral examination and sat in the front row in order to demonstrate her pride in him. Her son, however, refused to answer a single question during the exam; he would not allow her to possess him.[41]

The distinguishing characteristic of mothers of men driven by the hunger for political power is that they dominate their sons by making them into tools of their own dreams of power. It makes little difference whether, like Nixon's mother, they directly fuel a son's ambition or, like Hitler's, make him into their savior. In every case, such a mother does not love her son for his own sake but uses him as a tool in a secret struggle against the husband. Her hatred for the latter becomes an ever-present threat for the son, who could be rejected like the father if he no longer meets the mother's expectations. Hitler's mother enabled her son to live an idle life for two and a half years on the pension left by his father.[42] This kind of pampering is not a sign of maternal love; it simply shows the degree of disappointment with the husband. Mothers like this often hate their daughters, in whom they reject their own femininity.

A mother who, on the other hand, has ambivalent feelings about male superiority—for example, she may accept the male myth but not her husband—will pass on aspects of her skepticism to her son (or daughter), which can weaken his potential lust for power, perhaps even resulting in a "neurotic" constellation that makes him a "failure." We cannot be grateful enough for this maternal ambivalence, for these mothers will no longer transmit the male ideology but will be able to contribute (perhaps unconsciously) to the struggle against it.

Power-hungry people are not conscious of their inner emptiness. Unconscious of it in themselves, they cannot detect it in others. They see only the outer persona in order to avoid having to face their own emptiness. People whose inner emptiness is less pronounced are not so easily fooled. François Mitterrand, himself no disdainer of external display, is reported initially to have wanted to form a close relationship with Reagan; this desire "was tempered when they met by the discovery that 'there was nothing there to relate to' "![43]

Another president illustrates the way the struggle to gain power serves to compensate for collaborating in one's own debasement. After his sweeping election victory in 1964, Lyndon B. Johnson said, "I've been kissing asses all my life and I don't have to kiss them anymore."[44] At least he admitted to his self-betrayal.

THERE ARE TWO signs that betray the destructiveness powerful men conceal behind seeming amiability and benevolence:

First and foremost, self-pity passing itself off as suffering is a component of the fascistic personality, but it is not really linked to any particular ideology, for this personality type is to be found wherever power is exercised and can wear, for example, a democratic or communist mask with equal ease. It is not so much people's politics we should be concerned with as how honest they are with themselves as human beings.

Second, the unflagging proliferation of external enemies, which is an indication of the flight from inner phantoms and is an attempt to fuel and mobilize the latent hatred in the population, which has been produced by the ubiquity of self-betrayal.

The extent to which history is an expression of self-betrayal is determined by the extent to which gnawing self-hatred is present in the people who make it. The need of broad segments of the population to be delivered from this insidious self-hatred facilitates—especially in times of economic insecurity—the success of power-hungry political leaders, who for their part are trying to escape their own inner emptiness. They, then, are the "realists," who are the first to reject any psychological explanations for their actions. Since power is their reality, they have declared war on all psychologizing of history. The issue for them is not the rejection of psychology per se but the avoidance of their own truth. I have tried to show that "realism" is the attempt to live by denying any reality to an inner moral stance. Denial of the truth is the cornerstone on which such realism rests.

VII

The Psychopath
and Peer Gynt

SCHIZOPHRENICS SUFFER BECAUSE they are unable to accept the falseness of a self predicated on submission. Though longing for love, they recognize the hypocrisy of a love that must be bought at the price of self-surrender, and therefore they do their best to prove that the world cannot possibly love them. This enables them to escape the dangers of submitting and, at the same time, "save" their mother and father from having to shoulder any blame, for if they make themselves totally unlovable, then it is they who are responsible for their condition. Thus, they preserve their potential autonomy as well as the paradoxical hope of someday finding a loving link with humanity.

Unlike schizophrenics, there are those people I have described in preceding chapters who deny their pain and helplessness in order to gain the power that comes with approval. Their tactic is to opt for behavior that says: "Look! I am doing what you want, and therefore you must love me."

Clearly, there are numerous ways and degrees of escaping pain and helplessness. When, for instance, a child sees that adults are infuriated if the child reacts to pain with depression and withdrawal but are kindly disposed—because conscious of their power—if the child feigns tears, then a relationship to mother and father will be initiated that relies on power maneuvers. Children learn in this situation to simulate pain in order to manipulate those who inflict it.

Thus, insincerity and contempt for oneself and for adults come to underlie what one considers to be socially appropriate behavior. The child learns to influence the parents' expectations by playing with their hopes and soon figures out how to utilize the doubts lurking beneath parental authoritarianism. The "reality" of subsequent social interactions conceals the vengeful and destructive feelings directed against the love the child longed for but did not receive. The result is a pattern of behavior that characterizes the psychopath.

In preceding chapters, I have dealt primarily with the conformist. We find an intensification of that personality type in the psychopath, who exhibits extreme forms of destructiveness in the guise of conformity.

The psychiatrist Hervey Cleckley writes in his groundbreaking work *The Mask of Insanity* about a puzzling feature of psychopathic behavior. If the psychopath comes under psychological or psychiatric observation, the following picture emerges:

> In all the orthodox psychoses ... there is a more or less obvious alteration of reasoning processes or of some other demonstrable personality feature [such as delusions, hallucinations, and/or alogical thinking]. In the psychopath this is not seen. The observer is confronted with a convincing mask of sanity. All the outward features of this mask are intact; it cannot be displaced or penetrated by questions directed toward deeper personality levels. The examiner never hits upon the chaos sometimes found on searching beneath the outer surface of a paranoid schizophrenic. The thought processes retain their normal aspect under psychiatric investigation and in technical tests designed to bring out obscure evidence of derangement. Examination reveals not merely an ordinary two-dimensional mask but what seems to be a solid and substantial structural image of the sane and rational per-

sonality. . . . Furthermore, the observer finds verbal and facial expressions, tones of voice, and all the other signs we have come to regard as implying conviction and emotion and the normal experiencing of life. . . . All judgments of value and emotional appraisals are sane and appropriate when the psychopath is tested in verbal examinations.

Only very slowly . . . does the conviction come upon us that, despite these intact rational processes . . . we are dealing here not with a complete man at all but with something that suggests a subtly constructed reflex machine which can mimic the human personality perfectly. This smoothly operating psychic apparatus reproduces consistently not only specimens of good human reasoning but also appropriate simulations of normal human emotion in response to nearly all the varied stimuli of life. So perfect is this reproduction of a whole and normal man that no one who examines him in a clinical setting can point out in scientific or objective terms why, or how, he is not real. And yet we know or feel we know that reality, in the sense of full, healthy experiencing of life, is not here.[1]

Cleckley presents the hypothesis that this condition consists of a perceptual disturbance, "of an unawareness and a persistent lack of ability to become aware of what the most important experiences of life mean to others."[2] By this he means a lack of "the common substance of emotion" from which one's goals and responsibilities are derived. In the psychopath, the wholeness of experience is absent, blocked, or cut off. This corresponds exactly to that extreme state of outer-directedness I have described.

Schizophrenics attempt to retain their integrity by rejecting the outer forms and goals of life, whereas psychopaths escape their own center by a headlong rush into a realistic simulation of sanity, which is an indication of their extreme surrender to outer forms. This insistence on appearances is also a sign of contempt for the potential significance of an interior life capable of love. Since psychopaths attribute no real value to the forms they use to imitate life, they continually throw away what they have achieved through them.

In the article already cited, Ronald Steel refers to Nixon's self-justifying account of the Vietnam War: "His charge in this book [*No More Vietnams*] that the US won the great prize of victory in Vietnam and then threw it away has its ironic echo in Nixon's own life. It is as though he accuses others of doing with Vietnam what he himself did with the presidency."[3] Something similar appears to have occurred when Reagan, in 1986, used arms sales to Iran for the illegal financing of the Nicaraguan contras, thereby jeopardizing his presidency.

This kind of self-destructiveness very frequently accompanies the clinical picture of the psychopath. Unfortunately, when such people attain public power, we often excuse their self-destructiveness even though it harms us too. We want to come to their rescue because if we succeed in absolving them of guilt, we will also ease our own conscience.

Aside from its description in Cleckley's work, the nature of the psychopath as I interpret it has been presented primarily in fiction and drama. I have already cited in the second chapter the case of the murderer Niels Heinrich Engelschall in Jakob Wassermann's novel *The World's Illusion*. Wassermann's protagonist is familiar with all varieties of social behavior but knows nothing of love. His rage is directed indiscriminately against all of life. Joseph Conrad's work, too, is rich in descriptions of people who know how to mimic every feeling yet actually feel nothing but destructiveness.

I should now like to examine in some detail a drama by Henrik Ibsen that in my opinion demonstrates with extraordinary clarity the dynamics of the psychopath. It describes a son's submission to a mother who has sacrificed herself to her husband's world and manipulates her son for the sake of fortifying her flagging self-esteem. The author makes clear the link existing between the son's destructiveness and his largely unconscious hatred for his mother.

In his play in verse *Peer Gynt*, Ibsen portrays two opposing manifestations of womanhood—Aase, Peer Gynt's mother, who motivates him to strive for power; and Solveig, the woman who loves him and leads him to his inner self.[4] Aase has so completely internalized the ideology of masculine superiority and power that her own struggle for self-realization mirrors male self-deception. Solveig, on the other hand, is rooted in her inner self, where compassion and love hold sway, and has no need for male abstractions of power. In these two women, Ibsen intuitively depicts the poles I have described: the good and the bad mother.

Aase has ruined her son because, by destroying his ability to feel shame and guilt, she has made it impossible for him to see himself. The distinction between "feeling guilt" and "guilt feelings" is an important one: the source of the former is perceiving responsibility, whereas for the latter it is fear of those in authority. Aase excuses all her son's actions but at the same time belittles him whenever he wants to act independently. This ambivalence is part of Aase's strategy to make Peer bend to her will. In the very first scene of the play, she berates him for fighting (although it later becomes clear that she admires him for it at the same time):

AASE: Can you deny you were the ringleader
      In that shindy at Lunde, when you fought
      Like mad dogs. Wasn't it you who broke
      The arm of Aslak the smith? Or at least
      Put one of his fingers out of joint?
PEER: Who's been filling your ears with such rubbish?
AASE (*heatedly*): The crofter's wife heard him hollering.
PEER (*rubs his elbow*): No, that was me.
AASE: You?
PEER: Yes, mother. I was the one that took the beating.
AASE: What!
PEER: He's a nimble man.
AASE: Who's nimble?
PEER: Aslak the smith. I'm telling you, I know.

AASE: Shame upon you, shame! Now I must spit!
    That loafing sot, that swaggerer,
    That boozing sponge! Did you let him beat you?

    (*Weeps again.*)

    Many's the shame I've suffered, but this is the worst.
    Nimble, is he? Need you be weak?
PEER: Whether I bash a man or get bashed,
    You start moaning. (*Laughs.*) Now cheer up, mother—
AASE: What! Have you been lying again?
PEER: Yes, just this once. So dry your tears.

    (*Clenches his left fist.*)

    This was my tongs. With this I held the smith
    Bent double; my right fist was my hammer—
    . . . .
    Sweet, ugly little mother, you take my word.
    The whole parish shall honour you. Just wait
    Till I do something, something really big!
    . . . .
    I'll be King! Emperor!
AASE: God help me!
    Now he's losing the little wit he's got.

Aase's contempt for him is expressed vividly here, but so is her feeling that Peer is a part of herself and that she expects great things of him:

    Shut your gullet. You're out of your mind.
    Oh, it's true enough something might have come of you
    If you hadn't got lost in lies and twaddle.
    The Heggstad girl fancied you.
    You could have won her easily if you'd wanted—

When it's a matter of a bride for Peer, Aase urges him not to set any boundaries to his ambitions:

    Ah, Peer, my son, she's rich. The land's all hers.
    Just think. If you'd only put your mind to it

> You'd be wearing the bridegroom's coat,
> Not standing here black and tattered.

Yet when he decides to woo the girl, his mother curbs his initiative:

> While you were away
> In the western mountains, riding stags through the air,
> Mads Moen's got the girl.

But when Peer now persists and wants his mother to go with him to Ingrid's father and convince him to accept Peer as his son-in-law, Aase does not want to help him. She even threatens him, shouting:

> Never you fear! A grand character I'll give you!
> I'll tell them all about you, I'll tell them
> All your devilries—
> . . . .
> I won't stop
> Till the old man sets his dog on you like a tramp.

She then tries to stop him from going to Heggstad. Peer reacts by simply putting his mother on the millhouse roof, from which she cannot get down by herself, so that he can run off to Heggstad to Ingrid's wedding feast. Aase is afraid:

> Peer, take me down this instant!
> PEER: I would if I dared.
>
> (*Comes closer.*)
>
> Remember, sit still now. Don't kick
> Or start pulling down the tiles, or you'll hurt yourself.
> And maybe fall down.
> AASE: You brute!

But her anger soon turns to fear that he will come to grief.

The scene changes. We see Peer arriving at the wedding feast and hear him talking to himself:

> I'll go home to mother.
>
> (*Starts up the hill again, but stops and cocks an ear toward the fence.*)
>
> The dancing's begun!
>
> . . . .
>
> What a fine swarm of lasses!
> Seven or eight to every man!
> Oh, flames, I must go and join in the fun!
> But mother's up on the millhouse roof.
>
> (*His eyes are drawn toward the feast again. He jumps and laughs.*)
>
> Hey, how the dancers fly over the grass!
> By God, he's a boy on the fiddle! It laughs
> And splutters just like a waterfall.
> And oh, what a covey of glittering girls!
> Yes, flames, I must go and join in the fun!
>
> (*Leaps over the fence and goes down the road.*)

Here Peer displays what is found clinically in every psychopath: the deep split between overt tenderness and concern for his mother and simultaneous hatred for her.

The following case history of Milt as described by Hervey Cleckley serves as a parallel example of this phenomenon. Milt's parents were worried about him because he was unable to take anything seriously. He was often involved in adolescent pranks without ever learning from his mistakes. Nor did he seem to have any feeling of responsibility for the damage he caused. Each time he would apologize profusely, and he appeared to understand that he was in the wrong. When he was caught repeating the same act, he would "express his regret with the same charming politeness."[5]

Cleckley describes a significant incident: Once Milt's mother, who had just returned from the hospital after major surgery, had to go out to take care of a business matter, and Milt graciously offered to take her in the family car. As they were driving over a long bridge, the car suddenly came to a stop. Milt soon located the cause of the trouble, a blown fuse, and set off to get a replacement. He took leave of his mother affectionately and promised to be back within fifteen minutes. But more than an hour passed, and he did not reappear. His mother panicked, fearing that something had happened to Milt, and finally got a ride home from another motorist. She phoned two hospitals and had already sent her younger son to the garage Milt had said he was going to when Milt himself appeared, indignant that his mother had not waited for him. He had gotten the fuse, returned to the car, and driven home. Milt was immune to the reproach that he had been very inconsiderate by being gone for such a long time and had behaved irresponsibly. It turned out that initially he had hurried, but had then stopped at a cigar store to check the latest football scores. At this point, he recalled that a girl he knew lived nearby, and he went to see her, staying for approximately an hour although he had no special liking for the girl. From there he went to the garage.

"It is interesting to note," Cleckley writes, "that this conduct did not result from absentmindedness, from specific amnesia or confusion. . . . He was quite aware all through the episode of his mother waiting on the bridge and seems to have been free from any grudge or other impulse that would influence him deliberately to offend her or cause her hardship."[6] What strikes me as particularly interesting about this story is that it demonstrates that the psychopath "knows" what he is doing but lacks any awareness of the motivation for his conduct.

This case history illustrates the mimicry of those feelings that accompany what appears to be completely normal behavior. The psychopath's technique is to divert us from the perception of our own feelings, and this is done in essentially two ways. When someone like Milt acts annoyed, as he did when he got home, he does it so convincingly that we lose sight of the actual facts and of our own appraisal of the situation and begin to "feel" with him. We do not notice that his indignation, for instance, does not fit the real situation. The second method, linked to the first, consists of acting the role of the victim—the poor boy was abandoned by his mother! The strategy here is one of self-pity. Psychopaths simulate feelings to confuse us, so that we doubt our own feelings and perceptions and start to feel guilty.

When people like Milt are given psychiatric attention because the people living with them can no longer cope with their eccentric behavior and are concerned about their apparent lack of feelings, treatment is as a rule soon terminated because no illness can be diagnosed. Even professionals fail to see the split, no longer trust the integrity of their own perception—assuming such integrity exists—and are completely taken in by the psychopath's "sane" appearance.

Returning to *Peer Gynt*, we see the same dynamics unfold. Peer has gone to the wedding feast and is about to abduct the bride. Aase, who has been helped down from the millhouse roof by passersby, enters along with the smith, who wants to give Peer a thrashing:

AASE (*enters with a stick in her hand*): Is my son here?
      Wait till I get his pants down!
      I'll thrash the holy life out of him!
ASLAK (*rolls up his sleeves*): That stick's too puny for a fat lout like him.

      . . . . . .
      (*He spits on his hands and nods at* AASE.) Hang him!
AASE: What! Hang my Peer? Just you try!
      I've teeth and claws! Where is he?

(*Shouts across the yard.*)

Peer!

Then Peer is seen fleeing up the hillside with the bride. Aase shakes her fist at him as she cries:

> May God strike you down—!
>
> (*Shrieks in terror.*)
>
> Be careful!
> BRIDE'S FATHER (*enters bareheaded and white with rage*):
> Bride-rape! I'll have his life for this!
> AASE: I'll burn in Hell before you do!

Here Ibsen emphasizes the mother's rapid alternation between fury when her son does not fulfill her expectations and, conversely, seductive sweetness and concern. Peer's feelings toward women are such that he secretly values only what he has never experienced: true love. What he can have becomes worthless as soon as he possesses it. Therefore, he rejects Ingrid after seducing her:

> PEER: Get away from me!
> INGRID (*weeps*): After this! Where can I go?
> PEER: Anywhere you like.
> INGRID (*wrings her hands*): You have betrayed me!
> PEER: It's no good moaning. It's finished.
> INGRID: Our crime binds us. Our double crime.
> PEER: All memories belong to the Devil.
>   All women belong to the Devil.
>   Except one—
> INGRID: Which one?
> PEER: Not you.
> INGRID: Who is it, then?
> PEER: Go! Go back where you came from!
>   Quick! To your father!
> INGRID: You can't mean what you say.
> PEER: Can and do.
> INGRID: To seduce me, and then leave me!
> PEER: What wealth have you to offer me?

INGRID: Heggstad farm, and more besides.

.   .   .   .

PEER: When I see you, does the sun shine?
   Well!
INGRID: No, but—
PEER: What's all the rest, then? (*Turns to go.*)
INGRID (*steps in front of him*): Don't you know they'll hang
   you if you leave me?
PEER: All right!
INGRID: Your mind's made up, then?
PEER: Like stone.
INGRID: Very well. We'll see who wins.

   (*Goes down the path.*)

PEER (*is silent for a moment, then suddenly cries*): All memo-
   ries belong to the Devil!
   All women belong to the Devil!
INGRID (*turns her head and shouts scornfully up at him*): Ex-
   cept one!
PEER: Yes. Except one.

With short and powerful strokes, Ibsen portrays Peer's attempt to distort Ingrid's perception of what she has experienced. Like the psychopath, he knows how to arouse guilt
feelings and to obscure the actual situation. Ingrid, however,
remains true to her feelings. The audience, on the other hand,
tends to take Peer's side in this scene.

Peer not only has contempt for women but also rejects
responsibility for his actions. Another aspect of the psychopath also surfaces: self-destructiveness. Peer does what his
mother wants and, like Richard Nixon, turns his back on
what he has achieved. It might be said that he rejects Ingrid
because of his longing for the purity of Solveig, whom he
met before seducing Ingrid, but as we shall see he is only
using Solveig to avoid real involvement. Is not his self-
destructiveness a way of getting back at his mother?

Ibsen also describes Aase's relationship with her husband,

to whom she submitted at the sacrifice of her own self. There
is a clear connection between her submission and her compulsive need to entangle Peer in her fantasy world. As the
play unfolds, we see her searching for her son:

> Everything's against me. The world's angry!
> . . . .
> And the whole parish is shouting for his blood.
> Which they shan't have, for I can't live without him.
>
> . . . .
> Mind, when times were tough we stuck together,
> For my man had a tongue red for drink.
> An idler he was with his bragging, wasting our wealth,
> While I and my baby sat at home
> Trying to forget. What else could we do?
> For I was never a one for arguing.
>
> . . . .
> So we took to romancing of princes and trolls
> And all kinds of beasts. And stealing brides
> From their white wedding-beds. But who'd have thought
> Those daft ideas would have stuck in his head?

Many strands come together here: Aase's need to fuse herself with her son to make up for her lost self-esteem; her
contempt for her husband and her inability to stand up to
him; her search for forgetfulness, even making a virtue of it.
She makes Peer an accomplice in her fantasized attacks
against women (not men!), which is her way of taking revenge
on her own sex that she scorns as weak, in accordance with
the male myth of power. It is interesting that in Ibsen's play
Peer's father is an alcoholic, as were Hitler's and Reagan's.
From this background, then, emerges a power-hungry man.

In the next scene, we see Peer running impetuously on a
hillside; he feels wild and free, feels "alive." But the following lines reveal what kind of aliveness it is:

> The whole parish is after me in a mob!
> . . . .

This is better sport than bashing a smith!
This is life! I feel as strong as a bear!

(*Punches around and jumps in the air.*)

To smash and overturn! To dam the waterfall!
To strike! To wrench the fir up by the root!
This is life. It hardens and elevates.
To hell with all bloody lies!

Note how Ibsen shows that "conquering" nature has its roots in destructiveness. Peer is out to murder life in all its manifestations. And his mother absolves him of all guilt, as she did after he abducted and seduced Ingrid. He is not blamed for anything:

Ingrid came safely home in the end.
It's the Devil they ought to blame. He's the villain
And no-one else. He led my boy astray.

In the fourth act, which takes place on the southwest coast of Morocco, Peer, now a successful businessman, is basking in grandiose feelings:

My self—it is the army
Of wishes, appetites, desires,
The sea of whims, pretensions and demands,
All that swells here within my breast
And by which I, myself, exist.
But as Our Lord has need of common clay
To make Him omnipotent, so I need gold
To make me Emperor.

One morning he waxes enthusiastic at the spectacle and peace of nature and then immediately thinks of ways to gain power over it:

What a vast and limitless waste!
Far away over there an ostrich is strutting.

What is one to believe was God's intention
In creating all this emptiness and death?
This desert, devoid of all sources of life,
Burnt and yielding profit to no man.

. . . .

The sea's in the west behind me,
Dammed from the desert by a range of hills.

(*A thought strikes him.*)

Dammed? I wonder—? Those hills are narrow.
Dammed? A little dynamite, a canal,
And the waters would rush like a life-giving river
In through the gap and fill the desert.

. . . .

And in the midst of my sea, on a rich oasis,
I shall personally propagate the Norwegian race.

. . . .

A little money and I could do it!
A golden key to the gate of the sea!
A crusade against Death! That mean old skinflint
Shall open the sack he lies brooding on!

In the name of life he wants to sow the seeds of death, promoting death as though it were life. Was Hitler's dream of world conquest or Reagan's fantasy of Star Wars any different? Both claimed to be acting in the name of peace.

Peer Gynt hates life and goodness. In the play's fifth act, he is a worn-out old man on a ship taking him back to Norway, and he soliloquizes about some sailors on the ship whom he has been asked to help:

To have a home full of children; to be their joy.
To be always in the forefront of their minds.
To be followed on one's way by the thoughts of others—
There's no one who ever thinks of me.
Candles on the table! I'll put out those candles!
I'll find some way! I'll make them all drunk!
Not one of those fools shall go ashore sober.
They'll come home drunk to their wives and children.

They'll swear, and knock them about—all their love destroyed!
They'll frighten their loved ones out of their wits.

Meanwhile the sea grows stormier. A wreck is sighted with
people on board; Peer seems transformed: he wants to do
everything possible to rescue those in danger. As always, he
is playing with the hopes and expectations of others—and is
even admired for it:

PEER: Quick! Lower a boat!
CAPTAIN: She'd fill before we cast off. (*Goes forward.*)
PEER: Who cares about that?

(*To some of the crew.*)

                              If you're men, save them!
     You're not afraid of getting wet, are you?
BOATSWAIN: It's impossible in a sea like this.
PEER: They're screaming again. Look, there's a lull!
     You, cook! Will you try? I'll give you money!
COOK: Not if you gave me twenty pounds.
PEER: You dogs! You cowards! Don't you realise
     These men have wives and children at home?
     They are sitting, waiting for them—!

After the foundering ship has sunk, drowning all on board,
Peer says:

     There's no faith left among men any more.
     Christianity's only preached and written;
     There's little charity and less prayer.
     They've no respect for the powers above.
     On a night like this our Lord is dangerous.

     .   .   .   .

     I'm guiltless. On the Day of Judgment I can swear
     I stood ready and willing with money in my hand.

Soon Peer's ship sinks too, and he takes refuge on a capsized
dingy. The cook is beside him. After a violent struggle, Peer

pushes him into the water and cold-bloodedly watches him drown. Another person, the Strange Passenger, is suddenly at his side. Through him, Ibsen comments on Peer's inability to feel, which allows him to let the cook drown and try now to push the Strange Passenger into the water as well:

> STRANGE PASSENGER: My friend, have you even once a year
>   Known the true anguish of the soul?
> PEER: Of course one's afraid, when danger threatens—
>   But everything you say has another meaning.
> STRANGE PASSENGER: Yes, but have you once in life
>   Won the victory that only defeat can bring?

Finally reaching land, Peer chances upon a burial service, to which he pays hypocritical homage:

> Yes, the Church is the only true comforter.
> I haven't fully appreciated it before.
> But now I realise how good it is
> To be assured by the voice of authority:
> "As a man sows, so shall he reap."
> One must be oneself and look after oneself
> And one's own, in all things, whether great or small.
> If your luck runs out, at least you've the honour
> Of having lived your life in accordance with
> The best principles. . . .

Near the end of the play, Peer, sitting in the woods near the house where he grew up, which has now fallen into decay, becomes aware of his inner emptiness. He is peeling an onion, and he identifies each layer with one of the many roles he has played throughout his life:

> One must try them all, and choose the best.
> I've tried the lot. I started as Caesar
> And I've come right down to Nebuchadnezzar.
>
> . . . .

What a terrible lot of layers there are!
Surely I'll soon get down to the heart?

(*Pulls the whole onion to pieces.*)

No—there isn't one! Just a series of shells
All the way through . . .

Then he hears Solveig singing, and another memory is awakened in him. He turns deathly pale:

One who remembered—and one who forgot.
One who kept what the other has lost.
And the game can never be played again!
Oh, here was my Empire and my crown!

Peer cannot bear this truth, and he runs through the forest to
escape the images and thoughts besetting him. Ibsen presents
these in the form of "threadballs" rolling at his feet, dry
leaves, a whispering in the air, dewdrops, and broken straws.
They all address him, reproaching him for what he has left
undone:

THREADBALLS (*on the ground*): We are thoughts.
    You should have thought us.

    . . . .

WITHERED LEAVES (*flying before the wind*): We are a
    trumpet-call.
    You should have sounded us.

    . . . .

A WHISPERING IN THE AIR: We are songs.
    You should have sung us.
    A thousand times
    You have stifled and strangled us.
    In the mine of your heart
    We have lain and waited.
    We were never summoned.

    . . . .

DEWDROPS (*dripping from the branches*): We are tears
    You never wept.
    We could have melted
    The sharp ice-spears.
    Now they fester
    Deep in your breast.
    The wound has closed.
    Our power has gone.
    . . . .
BROKEN STRAWS: We are deeds
    You left undone.

Peer's running is in vain; he cannot escape himself any longer.

A Button Moulder now appears and wants to melt him down in his casting ladle, but Peer protests:

    To be melted, and to be Peer Gynt no more—
    It fills my soul with revulsion.
BUTTON MOULDER: But, my dear Peer, there's really no need
    To get so upset. You have never been yourself.
    What does it matter if you disappear?

The Button Moulder lets him get away, and when they meet again, Peer asks him:

    One question. What does it mean: "To be oneself"?
BUTTON MOULDER: That's a strange question, from a man
    Who a moment ago—
PEER: Come on, answer me!
BUTTON MOULDER: To be oneself is: to kill oneself.

This definition is strongly reminiscent of the words of Jakob Böhme, the seventeenth-century mystic, who writes, "Who dies not before he dies is ruined when he dies." This is the crux of the matter. People like Peer Gynt, who live in terms of appearances, are afraid to let go of their protective shell. Not until they "die," that is, stop playing roles, do they find they can be truly alive. Ibsen expands on this theme from an interesting perspective toward the end of the play: There are two ways that people can be themselves, a right way and a wrong way. Ibsen uses his character the Thin Person to introduce the simile of a photographic negative on which people are, so to speak, the opposite of what they could have been. With this image, he touches upon the central issue of the self: to find oneself means taking responsibility for oneself. Eldridge Cleaver, the black revolutionary who became an engaged citizen, is an outstanding example of a man who takes responsibility for his dark side. The Peer Gynts, however, who were never truly people in the first place, have, in Ibsen's words, "smudged themselves out." Peer recognizes this in the end when he cries out, "I was a dead man long before I died!"

Peer makes a last desperate attempt to escape both the Button Moulder and Solveig. In his despair, he asks the latter, "Where was my self, my whole self, my true self?" And now Ibsen brings about the seemingly impossible: the salvation of Peer's soul through the love he rejected. Solveig answers Peer:

> In my faith, in my hope, and in my love.
> PEER (*starts back*): What do you say? Hush! Now you speak in riddles!
> Ah! *You* are the mother to that child?
> SOLVEIG: Yes, I am. But who is its father?
> It is He Who forgives when the mother prays.
> PEER (*bathed in light, cries*): My mother! My wife! O, thou pure woman!
> O hide me in your love! Hide me! Hide me!

Ibsen clearly wants us to understand that the power of compassion overcomes the stern paternal taskmaster and is the antidote to the mythology of maleness. Solveig succeeds in reaching Peer with her compassion, with the result that he can finally stop running from himself.

Peer Gynt is the story of a man who tries all his life to find the empire he is supposed to rule over, only to discover in the end that it is nothing other than what he has always spurned: his own self. It is Ibsen's genius that he not only makes the correct diagnosis but also knows what the remedy is: taking responsibility for the self. As he wrote in a letter to Ludwig Passarge, the German translator of the play: "Everything that I have written is most minutely connected with what I have lived through, if not personally experienced; every new work has had for me the object of serving as a process of spiritual liberation and catharsis; for every man shares the responsibility and the guilt of the society to which he belongs."[7]

Peer Gynt does not at first glance seem "crazy" to us. He maintains his facade and is so successful in manipulating the inner contradictions of others to his own advantage that he can hardly abandon this strategy. The schizophrenic, on the other hand, attempts to reconcile contradictions, first of all in the mother, then in society.

Those whose feeling and thinking are directed—albeit unconsciously—toward manipulating others will always believe they are surrounded by enemies; they will construct a reality that corresponds to their inner cauldron of hate and vengefulness. These people's unconscious does not consist, as Freud thought, of repressed sexual drives but of self-hatred stemming from the loss of autonomy. Certainly, sexual conflicts play an important role, but if we direct our attention exclusively to sexuality and the aggressiveness accompanying it, we will lose sight of a deeper and more basic phenomenon—namely, the individual's contribution to the loss of his or her humanity. When self-betrayal is as radical as it is in the psychopath, the unconscious is marked by chaos, extreme vengefulness, and murderousness.

This chaotic condition is due to the fact that the unconscious is cut off from vital interactions between inner and outer sources of stimulation. The frequently observed reversal of hatred into "love" shows how little the interior world has to do with the exterior one, and vice versa. This split-off unconscious does not have the integrative force to bring about a unitary and balanced psyche. The so-called neurotic or the schizophrenic, as well as the creative personality, does have access to the unconscious, experiencing it in relationship to processes inside and outside the individual—not as something utterly alien and unconnected.

The two extremes of psychic disorder that I locate in the psychopath on the one hand and the schizophrenic on the other reflect different aspects of our reality. The schizophrenic's excess of suffering and helplessness is a parody of the inner world of feeling, whereas the psychopath's behavior is a parody of the rules of our everyday reality. The psychopath holds us so firmly to this outer reality that the inner one appears not to exist.

Schizophrenics try to arouse our compassion but reject it when we offer it because they want to prove that everyone is hypocritical. Psychopaths play on our expectations of success and security, which, once awakened, they then disappoint. Schizophrenics make themselves the object of our worst expectations, thereby becoming our sacrificial victims and insisting that they are responsible for it. In contrast, psychopaths escape all responsibility by confusing the issue and claiming our pity.

Among many others, Hitler and Reagan illustrate these psychopathic characteristics. Hitler promised his people Lebensraum and prosperity but visited death and destruction upon them. In the end, he blamed them for his defeat and showed nothing but contempt for them. On one occasion, for instance, on the grounds that the nation had "betrayed" him, he deliberately caused the death of the women and children who had taken refuge in Berlin's subways. And we have already discussed Reagan's contempt for people. His particular way of denying responsibility manifests itself in his parody of righteousness. He hides his devious and insincere behavior behind a mask of piety and innocence. For example, he invokes the spirit of the American Revolution and its heroes to distort the truth. During a press conference on February 21, 1985, he described the Nicaraguan contras as "the moral equal of our Founding Fathers." He gave this accolade to murderous mercenaries whose leaders had been members of Somoza's corrupt and brutal National Guard and who were cited by Americas Watch for their systematic violation of human rights.[8]

The crucial question concerning human development has to do with how individuals deal with vulnerability. Did they pass through it and experience its proximity to dissolution and death? Did they find out that the death of outer forms of the self is not the same as the death of the self? Or did they choose submission in order to participate in the power oppressing them? Paradoxically, one must experience the terror of dying in order to be truly alive. If we never dared to do this, we will continually be in fear of the life we have never lived.

I shall try to illustrate this. The first discontinuity to occur in the development of the self is the transition from a state in which the order of things is determined by someone else to a frightening state of chaos and aloneness and then to an order of one's own.[9] In his book *The Divided Self*, R. D. Laing has drawn attention to an observation Freud made years ago, which is hidden in a footnote appearing in *Beyond the Pleasure Principle*. Freud describes a one-and-a-half-year-old child's peekaboo game that shows how mastery of life and death may come about. It involves the transformation from being somebody in the mother's eyes to becoming somebody in one's own. This child would throw whatever he got hold of as far from him as he could. He also liked to play with a reel that had a string tied around it. Instead of pulling it along behind him, he would throw the reel over the edge of his crib and then gleefully pull it up again by the string. In the footnote, Freud tells of a discovery the child made: once when his mother was away for several hours, the boy "found a method of making *himself* disappear. He had discovered his reflection in a full-length mirror that did not quite reach to the ground, so that by crouching down he could make his mirror-image 'gone.' "[10]

Referring to this incident, Laing writes: "Freud suggests that both games are to be understood as attempts to master the anxiety of a danger situation [the mother's absence] by repeating it again and again in play. If this is so, the fear of being invisible, of disappearing, is closely associated with the fear of his mother disappearing. It seems that loss of the mother, at a certain stage, threatens the individual with the loss of his self.... [I]n overcoming or attempting to overcome the loss or absence of the real other in whose eyes he lived and moved and had his being, he becomes another person to himself who could look at him from the mirror."[11] Thus, the seemingly banal game of peekaboo can help the child to experience himself as a separate individual.

How close this experience can be to the experience of psychological death is revealed by the novelist Ellen Glasgow in her autobiography *The Woman Within*: around the age of one or two, she had a terrifying experience that made her aware of being separate from her mother. Here, too, the feeling of being about to die is brought about by the "absence" of the mother. Although she was sitting in a rocking chair holding Ellen, her mother momentarily withdrew her attention from her child, who experienced this as withdrawal.[12] (The importance of eye contact between mother and child has been investigated by George Victor and also by me.[13]) For Ellen Glasgow, however, this terrifying incident constituted the decisive experience that made her discover her own self: "Moving forward and backward [she was being rocked in her mother's arms], I open my eyes and look up at the top windowpanes.... I see a face without a body staring in at me, a vacant face, round, pallid, grotesque, malevolent. Terror ... stabbed me into consciousness.... Convulsions seized me, a spasm of dumb agony. One minute, I was not; the next minute, I was. I felt. I was separate. I could be hurt. I had discovered myself. And I had discovered, too, the universe apart from myself."[14]

It appears that becoming separate is possible only at the cost of the death of the earlier merged self. The transition to a genuine self of one's own cannot take place without pain. The fear of this pain is what makes us submit to authority, and whether or not we opt for power shows what kind of person we are.

The psychopathic personality can develop along two different lines. There are those who submit to power but do not strive to possess it themselves. Apparently, a sense of participation in or fusion with the source of power satisfies them. There are also those who want to exercise power and employ violence directly.

The submissive ones envy the "strong" and unconsciously wish to replace them, but this only intensifies their efforts at fusion. When their idols fall, however, their murderous hatred for those they formerly idolized comes to the surface. In all likelihood, the extent to which a mother makes it impossible for her child to feel guilt determines the intensity of the child's drive to wield power. Both types, however, belong to a world, as Ronald V. Sampson puts it, "peopled by creatures unable to live outside the security of a coercive culture."[15]

The experience described by Ellen Glasgow, on the other hand, strikes me as prototypical of the breakthrough to an autonomous, inner-directed self.

If, in the course of our development, there occurs a division between inner- and outer-directedness, this also has implications for the image we have of our own body. Paul Schilder was one of the first to place our perception of our body into the context of the totality of our interactions; he writes that our "body-image is the result of social life."[16] Correspondingly, the image we have of our body and the way we relate to it reflect either the integration or dissociation of the inner and outer spheres of life.

Doris Beckord provides convincing corroboration of this in her pioneering study of the body images and bodily experiences of pregnant women. She was able to demonstrate that a direct connection exists between their perception of their body and their subsequent openness to the needs of the child. A pregnant woman who perceives and experiences positively the changes in her body primarily via "bathyesthesia," that is through visceral and kinesthetic sensations, also perceives the fetus from within, as it were; she experiences its first movements as a sign of a separate being and is later able to react empathically to the needs of the newborn infant. In contrast, women who have repressed their visceral sensations have a predominantly visual impression of their body; they see it from outside and during pregnancy are concerned mainly with their appearance and their sexual attractiveness. For them, the fetus is something alien, which they struggle to visualize. They experience the delivery less positively and are not able to initiate body contact with their baby as spontaneously. They feel overtaxed and can understand the baby's crying only in terms of hunger and illness because they have difficulty empathizing with its needs for closeness, security, and being held.[17]

Beckord emphasizes that the perception of one's body and its inner processes is strongly influenced by societal factors. A culture that places great value on externals shuts off access to somato-visceral sensitivity, and this has important consequences for mothering. A mother, for example, who bases her self-esteem on her sexual attractiveness to the male, cannot recognize and respect her child's intrinsic value. She will use the child for her own power games, perhaps excessively fueling his or her ambition. Only if the mother can question her own ambition will the child have a chance to lead an independent life. Here we can see how the stage is set at birth for a child to be pushed into an inner or outer direction, toward love or toward power; it is the mother's attitude and her own developmental history that exert their influence on the child as early as the prenatal and perinatal stages.

It is significant that one of the more recent studies of psychiatric disorders finds substantial differences in the statistics for men and women. Because the myth of maleness has an insidious tenacity that prevents men from being in touch with their inner self, psychopathology in men is far more frequently expressed by asocial behavior than in women, who are more likely to struggle with themselves. Eight times more men than women become violent when they are no longer able to deal with their problems. Four times more men than women resort to alcohol abuse or drug dependency. On the other hand, almost twice as many women as men suffer from depression and more than twice as many women are diagnosed as schizophrenic.[18] When faced with psychological difficulties, women internalize their struggle, whereas men, cut off from their inner self, externalize theirs in a vengeful way and seek solutions outside themselves.

Therefore, many more men than women become psychopaths. Their myth of strength fuels an insanity that masks itself as sanity and, therefore, has long been unrecognized as the danger it is.

VIII

Insanity as Way of Life, Insanity as Protest

DESTRUCTIVENESS IS THE direct expression of the insanity of those devoted exclusively to "reality," although ideological disguises usually obscure this fact. The insanity of these "realists" consists in their denial of humaneness under the guise of concern for human beings. They know how to present a human face but have none of the corresponding feelings. Their inner self is a cauldron of vengefulness and murderousness; in place of a living self there is only emptiness. To escape this emptiness and their inner chaos, they must attack life around them, for only this gives them a sense of aliveness.

The success of the "realists" is based not only on their skill in making themselves indispensable as leaders but also on the obedience of those who need such leaders in order to surrender their self and whose need to conform reduces their whole being to the function of obeying rules. In their obsessive adherence to the letter of laws and regulations, they destroy the reality of the world of feelings, with the result that they do not need to acknowledge their own destructive impulses. These people often find their niche within bureaucratic structures, where in the name of law and order they can demolish feelings while considering themselves morally right.

These conformists are the foot soldiers of the psychopathic leaders who are pushing the world toward the abyss. This collaboration makes the situation even more dangerous. An example of such collaboration: in 1940 an official in the German Department of Justice wrote to the minister of justice on the subject of euthanasia, urging him to bring all his influence to bear on legalizing the lawless killing of psychiatric and handicapped patients in the Third Reich. The honor of the entire system of justice was at stake, he said. Conscience means nothing here, conscientiousness everything, as Roland Kirbach bitterly notes.[1] The willingness to place rules above life makes the unholy alliance between conformist and psychopath possible. Their collaboration occurs in different ways, three of which I would like to discuss here.

Reductionism: The reduction of events to only one given dimension in order to block the appropriate emotional reactions was a daily practice in the United States during the Vietnam War. The Talk of the Town column in the *New Yorker* of May 29, 1971, describes a new kind of listing used to indicate the progress in the "pacification" of South Vietnamese villages:

> The list included the following achievements: 5,269 Medcap patients, 2,200 litres of chemicals used for defoliation, 250 acres cleared by bulldozers, 20,860 sheets of roofing issued to 1,156 families, 524 hours of psychological warfare by loudspeaker, and 4 music concerts conducted. As a means of arriving at a quick judgment on a complicated matter, such a list has advantages that are obvious. It is simple, precise and objective. Vague, intangible questions that never can be answered satisfactorily are avoided—questions such as: Did the villagers enjoy the 524 hours of psychological warfare by loudspeaker? Did that help to win them over to our side?

What is the proper balance between "music concerts conducted" and "litres of chemicals used for defoliation"? Is 2,200 litres of chemicals to 4 concerts right, or should it be 4 litres of chemicals to 2,200 concerts? Should any litres of chemicals be sprayed or any concerts be conducted at all by us in Vietnam?

The article continues with further examples of how events can be bureaucratized, giving an entirely new dimension to the reality of the lives involved, a bureaucratic reality unrelated to the world of suffering and joy:

Another list having to do with pacification added a refinement. It listed the tasks necessary for the pacification of a village and also listed "maximum number of points" that could be won for full accomplishment of each task. Some of the tasks, together with their maximum point score, were as follows: "V.C. local/main force units destroyed or driven out, 15 points; Census completed, 2 points; V.C. infrastructure discovered, destroyed, or neutralized, 8 points; Census Grievance Teams completed interviewing each family, 2 points; Principal grievance completely processed, 3 points." . . . When the people in charge have given themselves a score for each task, they add up the figures to get the score for the whole village. This score, together with the scores of the other villages in the country, is fed into a computer to produce one big score, which is given out as the progress in pacification to date.

As if this were not enough, several other lists are cited, including one that contains then President Nixon's personal contacts with leaders "from every area of American life: from labor, more than 30 such contacts; racial minorities, almost 30 such contacts; campus representatives, more than 50 such contacts; businessmen, more than 150 such contacts. . . . More than 13,000 guests enjoyed the Nixons' hospitality at 132 dinners. . . ." The *New Yorker* article comments on the impact of such lists; they "have become an invaluable new tool for coping with the world. The baffling interconnectedness of things is dissolved at a stroke, and phenomena are made to line up in a neat row followed by a number. The intellectually stymieing disproportion between one thing and another . . . is eliminated. The tiresome obligation of deciding whether something is 'right' or 'wrong' is likewise lifted." I have quoted at such length because these passages show with striking clarity how reality can be reduced to externalities in the name of "realism." The people responsible for doing this have no connection to real needs and real feelings, yet they determine how events are presented and how we are supposed to perceive them. And most of us are completely satisfied with this reduced reality because it permits us to ignore the uncomfortable stirrings within us.

Banalization: Trivializing or banalizing events is another method of cutting off the feelings they might arouse. Reducing life to insignificant statistics is one way of banalizing it; subjecting it to the reign of technology is another way, for this is the easiest means for people to avoid accountability for their actions.

The most devastating example of this abdication is undoubtedly the technological advances of modern warfare, which have turned war into something casual and acceptable. In the past, those who did the killing also had to be prepared to die themselves, but today they use such highly sophisticated weaponry that they are scarcely aware that they are killing; at the same time, they are at little personal risk. War can now be waged in such a manner that killing need not enter one's consciousness. This banalization makes it possible for a U.S. intelligence official to state that a U.S. invasion of Nicaragua "would be as easy as 'falling off a log.' "[2] It never occurred to this man that killing human beings would be part of the undertaking. I cite this remark because it was made by a man who has great influence on the National Security Council.

The Strategy of Dissociation: President Reagan concluded his speech before the General Assembly of the United Nations in observance of its fortieth anniversary in 1985 with what the *New Yorker* called a "profoundly moving and yet strangely untethered metaphor." He recalled a heartrending scene that had occurred several days after the terrible Mexican earthquake a month earlier. Rescue workers searching for victims buried under the rubble of the Juarez Hospital had heard faint sounds and succeeded in recovering three still-living newborn babies. "Amidst all that hopelessness and debris," Reagan said, "came a timely and timeless lesson for us all. We witnessed the miracle of life."[3]

The *New Yorker*'s comment: "We've characterized this concluding flourish in the President's speech as strangely untethered because it didn't seem to grow out of anything in the speech. . . . [A]n audience of diplomats [was] gathered from around the world and waiting for some glimmer of hope regarding the position of the United States in the principal crisis facing the world today—the possibility of a sudden acceleration in nuclear-arms procurements, and the greatly magnified threat of nuclear annihilation. . . . In this context, the rhetorical flourish concluding the speech—that set piece about the infants being rescued from the shambles—seemed untethered."[4]

Naturally, Reagan's description was heart wrenching in and of itself. But he used it to divert our attention from the threat of nuclear destruction that concerns us all. I have already described such diversionary tactics in previous chapters as a hallmark of psychopathic behavior. Psychopaths destroy the connection between events and the feelings they arouse in us. Or they shift our attention to a minor yet strongly affect-laden detail, thereby making us question our perception of the situation and causing us to doubt the validity of our feeling—in the case just cited, that the nuclear threat is more important than the miraculous rescue of the three babies. Anyone who insists on calling attention to the discrepancy between the moving rescue of the babies and the magnitude of the problem facing the world risks being branded as unfeeling.

Therefore, it is not the least bit surprising that the dissociation of feelings prevails as long as political leaders create an atmosphere that undermines the human capacity for integration. One of their favorite methods of doing this is to manipulate memory. In his novel *The Book of Laughter and Forgetting*, Milan Kundera writes that "the struggle of man against power is the struggle of memory against forgetting."[5]

Of course, if this struggle cannot take place at all because official information has already preprogrammed dissociation, remembering is automatically impossible. More than ten years after the end of the Vietnam War, Joseph Lelyveld talked with young Americans across the country about the war and found that their impressions of it were very vague. He presented a series of names to a Sunday-school class in Clayton, Missouri: McNamara, Ho Chi Minh, the Chicago Seven, Thieu, and Ky. The members of the class, all high-school juniors and seniors, could identify none of them. On another occasion, a young woman Lelyveld talked to at Fort Benning, Georgia, who was preparing for airborne training, said she thought the United States had won the war and was very surprised when Lelyveld told her it had not.[6]

The paradox here is that we live in a world in which the volume and speed of communication of information are greater than ever before. Although it is more accessible than ever, it is presented only in fragments, without being integrated into the totality of life. Thus, it has also become a rapidly perishable commodity. The young people Lelyveld questioned were ignorant not because they lacked access to information but because the available information lacked all connection to the pain and suffering in their everyday lives. That is why the students could not see that the events of the Vietnam War had something to do with them. People living under a totalitarian regime are far more alert and eager for information, because they must go to great efforts to obtain it.

Those who distort our perception of reality as something whole by leaving out the human dimension do this not only because they intentionally wish to deceive us but because they are afraid of integrating their inner world with the outer one. Integration would threaten their apparent but precarious balance, behind which psychosis lurks. And their fear is justified: rejection of the inner self, denial of the feeling of helplessness, and lust for power increase their self-rejection and, at the same time, intensify their inner emptiness, so that they have no choice but to step up their pursuit of power. In order to rationalize this, they *must* separate thinking and feeling from each other.

The pursuit of public power is a way of maintaining this inner split. The people involved in this pursuit seek power not for its own sake but to have something to hold on to in order not to fall apart. Therefore they can brook no compromise. Every further attempt to dominate increases their inner emptiness and necessarily produces a heightened need for domination. If one treats such people deferentially, they will interpret accommodation as a sign of weakness, for equality does not exist for them. For them there is only dominating or being dominated. They have learned the lessons of their childhood well: inflicting pain is an instrument of control; therefore, only power and violence count. Anything else would force them to confront the cowardice of their own early submission to pain. That is why any accord reached with them provokes further effort on their part to wield power more ruthlessly.

Nothing short of cataclysmic failure stops these people. By that time, however, it may be too late to prevent terrible consequences for all of us. Yet it is only with the total collapse of their "reality" that such people are likely to fall apart, for their exclusive involvement with the outer world protects them from their inner chaos. Their breakdown,

should it occur, is psychotic in the sense of a total disintegration. They have no center, only rage, and many can "save"
themselves only by suicide.

The breakdown of a psychopath differs fundamentally
from that of a schizophrenic, who attempts to preserve his or
her inner integrity by withdrawing from a world perceived as
hypocritical and evil. This attempt inevitably fails because
integration would involve exchange with the real world. The
sad yet admirable fact about the schizophrenic is, as Martti
Siirala puts it, that "to fall ill schizophrenically represents
not only a particular kind of weakness . . . but also a special
capacity to react totally to poisonous aspects of man's coexistence."[7] By this weakness Siirala means an inability to
oppose openly and directly the dissociated nature of our
civilization.

The psychotic type, on the other hand, denies both the
cause of our suffering and the contradictions that intensify it.
Psychotics, according to my use of the term, live totally cut
off from their inner world. If they do break down, their
overwhelming hatred will erupt—or at least their fear will
surface—but they cannot bring themselves to confront its
source. A breakdown often occurs when "failure" is experienced for the first time—in men, for example, as a function
of hormonal changes brought about by aging. The loss of
sexual potency confronts them concretely with the discrepancy between the reality of life in its fullness and their own
diminished one. This holds true for women as well. The
mania that so often characterizes this condition is an attempt
to perpetuate a hallucinated power. Siirala refers to this as an
attempt "to be a master of the law of life": "with extreme
adroitness [the patient] sweeps over all criticisms and judgments, as the laws valid for others do not apply to him."[8]

It is quite another matter with schizophrenics. In her autobiographical account, Barbara O'Brien shows us the nature
of the schizophrenic's struggle to preserve integration. She
describes the different selves in her past, which developed

entirely independently of one another. One self was grounded in her striving for autonomy; this self she kept out of sight, but it continued to exist. Another self lived in and adapted to the external world. To a certain extent, then, her biography contains elements of the "schizophrenic" as well as the "conformist" course of development. Her description of how she coexisted with her other selves makes her story illuminating:

> I was, like all children, no conformist. And like most people, I grew up to be the model of conformist adult. The only difference I can see between myself and most people is that in the process of maturing I learned early to live separately in different compartments. I became, in my early teens, a departmentalized child. . . . I was an ordinary enough child but I had some oddities. Because I was also a gregarious, adaptable child, eager to become an accepted part of my community, the oddities learned early to manifest themselves in safe places.[9]

In school, for example, she found unorthodox methods of solving mathematical problems. Because she always arrived at the correct answers, she was not criticized for being "odd." Sometimes her teachers even showed her off for the original way she came up with her solutions. "It was a safe department in which to be different."[10] In general, she had less success with her English compositions. When she was thirteen, she wrote a short story about a girl who decides that "there is no God as the picture of God is shaped by religious training," only to discover Him again through observing "the laws and rules of nature."[11] These were, of course, unusual ideas, and they aroused suspicion. But Barbara entered her story in a contest and won—because the judges were from outside her community.

O'Brien describes what was expected of people in her community after they finished high school or college: "You went to work for a company and you stayed with the same company until you married or became pregnant or died. You advanced in the company step by step, until you reached your top level.... You were expected to adjust to your company as you adjusted to the community. At my company, I adjusted well until I came up against something suddenly ... which [my adjusted self] couldn't handle."[12] Her inner self was of no help either, since it was not accessible to her because she had "buttoned it up," as she puts it.

What she came up against was ruthless power, which disregarded the values and standards that had been the basis for her adjustment and that she had accepted as true. Because she had "buttoned up" her inner self out of fear of rejection, it could break out only in hallucinatory form. At this point, her outer self collapsed. This happened the day after she left her job:

> When I awoke they were standing at the foot of my bed looking like soft fuzzy ghosts. I tried feeling the bedclothes. The sensation of feeling was sharp. I was awake and this was real.
>
> The boy was about twelve years old, handsome, and with a pleasant, relaxed smile. The elderly man was impressive: solid, conservative, a reliable man with built-in rules. The third was a real weirdo with hair three inches too long, black, straight, and limp, and with a body that was also long and limp. The face didn't belong with the body or the hair: the features were fine and sensitive, the expression, arrogant and unbending.
>
> The elderly man suddenly cleared his throat. "It is necessary for the good of all concerned that you get to know Hinton better." He turned and looked at the weirdo.
>
> I was positive that I had never seen that face before. The elderly man apparently sensed my thoughts. "You know him well," he said; "you used to know him better."[13]

Hinton was obviously Barbara O'Brien's repudiated inner self. She now began a journey on which she ultimately found her way back to wholeness through experiencing the hallucinations of her inner and outer world. She gained the strength to accept life in its evil as well as its humane dimensions. "The largest part of my hallucinations were concerned with learning the ways of the Hook Operators [the representatives of power realism] and learning how to fight them. Insanity was, for me, a training program, accompanied by escape from actual stress [she gave up her job and entered therapy] until I could gain what I needed psychologically to face the same stress in actuality."[14]

What she learned was how to unravel the complex ways in which she had rejected her own self and had accepted society's denial of her inner life. Her initial hallucination, described above, revealed her inner strength as well as the contempt with which she repudiated this strength: Hinton's "features were fine and sensitive, [his] expression, arrogant and unbending"; he was a "real weirdo." Hinton represented "a portion of mind that was prominent in childhood and which had been buried partly in adulthood."[15]

O'Brien's account continues: "Looked at in a certain light, there was much in my prior sanity which was not particularly stupid. Individuals adjust, if they are adaptable, to the mold of the community of which they are a part. In adjusting by departmentalizing [dissociating], I made a cautious, even cowardly, but not unintelligent adjustment to the community of which I was a part . . . I succeeded in adjusting well. . . . I used, for all I was worth, the qualities that were acceptable in the community and departmentalized what was not acceptable to areas where they could fit and would be accepted." She modifies this hypocrisy a few sentences later: "I departmentalized, burying elements inside of me which should never have been buried and as a consequence lost wholeness to gain acceptance for a part of me. Had I had the courage to be myself, I certainly would never have been called neurotic but at the worst, different. But 'different' is a criticism and one to which I had become extremely sensitive."[16]

This is the crucial difference between a person like O'Brien and those who travel the straight path to schizophrenia. The

latter never relinquish their inner self, which is why their illness evolves very gradually instead of breaking out suddenly.
In this regard, O'Brien's account gives us insight into the development of psychosis in an outer-directed person; it also
demonstrates, however, that both types of development—
toward outer-directedness and inner-directedness—can, to a
certain degree, proceed side by side in the same person. The
suddenness of a psychotic break indicates that at one time the
person who undergoes it made a basic decision to strive for
success and to participate in power.

Here, I believe, lies the diagnostic key for differentiating
between the two developmental directions I have proposed:
on the one hand, the long and insidious development leading
to increasing withdrawal from the social context and, on the
other, the sudden, precipitous break with social reality. In
the first case, we find individuals who struggle from earliest
childhood against surrendering to a reality that mocks their
longing for genuine love. In the second, we find those who
attempt to conform to social reality at the cost of their inner
truth. They collapse when outer reality no longer sustains
them because its contradictions have become too obvious
and crass. Their breakdown is clearly different from the so-
called disintegration of the schizophrenic, which is essentially an attempt at integration. Because schizophrenics
withdraw from the outer world in order not to have to
submit to its claim to power, it is difficult to recognize the
integrative aspect of their illness, especially if it is in an
advanced stage. Since they see every social interaction as
linked to the threat of having to submit, schizophrenics increasingly eliminate their contacts with the external world
and denude them of all meaning. In the end, schizophrenics
present us with the picture of a living death, a willed emptiness. But this is also an expression of their truthfulness and
their protest against a fundamentally inhumane reality.

The others, the would-be conformists, see a threat in the
very thing schizophrenics want to preserve for themselves.

To varying degrees, they try to escape pain, which they do not want to accept as a meaningful aspect of human experience and with which they are unable to come to terms. Because they, in order to avoid this pain, have capitulated to the power structures of external reality, genuine humaneness and the stirrings of their dissociated inner self become a source of anxiety for them. For these stirrings remind them of the autonomous impulses that were sacrificed because they stood in the way of conforming. The more pronounced the dissociation, the greater the anxiety. When the supportive facade of such people collapses, a breakdown of the personality occurs, which is basically different from the schizophrenic's withdrawal and self-impoverishment. That is what happened to Barbara O'Brien. Her case shows, too, that a breakdown can afford an opportunity for integration and new growth, providing there are still remnants of the autonomous self, even though encapsulated.

I use the term "psychosis" exclusively to describe the disorders of an externally derived self, not to describe schizophrenia. Psychotic behavior is characterized by the lack of attempts at synthesis and integration. Schizophrenia, on the other hand, is a struggle for integration that fails because of a lack of the strength to live one's inner truth in a hostile societal context. For this reason, the symptoms of schizophrenia will always have meaning. The symptoms of psychosis, as I understand it, have none; they are only an expression of hatred and destructive rage.

Schizophrenics' symptoms are messages they have encoded out of fear of not being understood. If we decode these messages, if we make an effort to understand them, then they can help us penetrate the fog created by those psychopaths who are in the seats of power and who have forced upon us a diminished view of reality. But as Abraham Lincoln once put it, "You may fool all the people some of the time; you can even fool some of the people all the time; but you can't fool all of the people all the time." Listening to those whose "insanity" is their protest will help us recognize more clearly those who are trying to fool us with their "realism." Once we have understood that their disguised destructive rage is nothing other than an escape from inner chaos and emptiness, we can identify their psychosis for what it is. Then the power they have over us will vanish.

This also will help us to gain a better understanding of the problem of good and evil. Where the inner world of feeling is split off, there will also be found only a split-off "morality" without any real influence on our actions. Because this kind of morality promotes the suppression of the autonomous self, it becomes itself a source of the evil it supposedly is combating. Truly responsible actions and genuine humaneness are possible only if there is an autonomous self that integrates the internal and external worlds. In this possibility lies the hope for our future.

Notes

Preface

1. Martti Siirala, "Was macht Gewalt bösartig?" (Paper delivered to the Deutsche Psychoanalytische Gesellschaft, Berlin, 13 November 1985).

2. Sigmund Freud, *Civilization and Its Discontents*, vol. 21 of *The Standard Edition of the Complete Psychological Works of Sigmund Freud*, trans. and ed. James Strachey (London: The Hogarth Press and the Institute of Psychoanalysis, 1981). Erich Fromm, *The Anatomy of Human Destructiveness* (New York: Holt, Rinehart and Winston, 1973).

3. Arno Gruen, *The Betrayal of the Self: The Fear of Autonomy in Men and Women*, with Preface by Gaetano Benedetti and Foreword by Ashley Montagu, trans. Hildegarde and Hunter Hannum (New York: Grove Press, 1988).

4. Michael Polanyi, *Personal Knowledge: Towards a Post-Critical Philosophy* (Chicago: Univ. of Chicago Press, 1960), 6.

Chapter I. The Denial of Reality in the Name of Realism

1. Gustav Bychowski, "Struggle against the Introjects," *International Journal of Psycho-Analysis* 39 (1958).

2. Arno Gruen, *Der frühe Abschied: Eine Deutung des Plötzlichen Kindstodes*, with Foreword by Ashley Montagu (Munich: Kösel, 1988).

3. Gaetano Benedetti, *The Psychotherapy of Schizophrenia* (New York: New York Univ. Press, 1987). Bruno Bettelheim, *The Empty Fortress: Infantile Autism and the Birth of the Self* (New

York: Free Press, 1967). Arno Gruen and Jirina Prekop, "Das Festhalten und die Problematik der Bindung in Autismus: Theoretische Betrachtungen," *Praxis der Kinderpsychologie und Kinderpsychiatrie* 7 (1986). Ronald David Laing, *The Divided Self: A Study of Sanity and Madness* (Chicago: Quadrangle Books, 1960). These works indicate that the "living death" of those suffering from autism and schizophrenia is the consequence of recurrent confrontations with the pain of rejection.

4. Henry Miller, *The Time of the Assassins: A Study of Rimbaud* (New York: New Directions, 1962), 104.

5. Carol F. Hoover, "Prolonged Schizophrenia and the Will," *Journal of Humanistic Psychology* 11 (1971).

6. H. Miller, Ibid.

7. Eric Aronson and Shelley Rosenbloom, "Space Perception in Early Infancy: Perception within a Common Auditory-Visual Space," *Science* 172 (11 June 1971).

8. Barbara and Arthur Gelb, *O'Neill* (New York: Harper & Row, 1973), 870.

9. Martti Siirala, *From Transfer to Transference* (Helsinki: Therapeia Foundation, 1983), 115. See also notes 27, chapter III, and 8, chapter VIII.

10. E. Shaheen et al., "Failure to Thrive: A Retrospective Profile," *Clinical Pediatry* 7 (1968). Margaretha A. Ribble, *The Rights of Infants: Early Psychological Needs and Their Satisfaction* (New York: Columbia Univ. Press, 1943). Gruen, *Der frühe Abschied.*

11. Harry Stack Sullivan, *The Interpersonal Theory of Psychiatry* (New York: W. W. Norton, 1953), 72.

12. Aarne Siirala, *Divine Humanness* (Philadelphia: Fortress Press, 1970), 123.

13. Sigmund Freud, *Three Essays on the Theory of Sexuality*, vol. 7 of *The Standard Edition of the Complete Psychological Works of Sigmund Freud*, trans. and ed. James Strachey (London: The Hogarth Press and the Institute of Psychoanalysis, 1953). *Beyond the Pleasure Principle*, vol. 18 of *Standard Edition* (1961). *New Introductory Lectures on Psycho-Analysis*, vol. 22 of *Standard Edition* (1971).

14. Arno Gruen, "Autonomy and Compliance: The Fundamental Antithesis," *Journal of Humanistic Psychology* 16, no. 3 (1976): 61.

15. M. Bertini et al., "Intrauterine Mechanisms of Synchronization: In Search of the First Dialogue," *Totus Homo* 8 (1978).

16. T. C. Schneirla, "An Evolutionary and Developmental Theory of Biphasic Processes Underlying Approach and Withdrawal," in *Nebraska Symposium on Motivation*, ed. Marshall R. Jones (Lincoln, Neb.: Univ. of Nebraska Press, 1959).

17. Jirina Prekop, "Frühkindlicher Autismus," *Offenes Gesundheitswesen* 44 (1982).

Chapter II. Self-Hatred as the Origin of Destructiveness

1. Neal Ascherson, "The 'Bildung' of Barbie," *The New York Review of Books*, 24 November 1983.

2. James R. Cameron, "Parental Treatment, Children's Temperament, and the Risk of Childhood Behavior Problems," *American Journal of Orthopsychiatry* 47 (1977). Arno Gruen, "Maternal Rejection and Children's Intensity: Implications for Sex Differences in Affective Development," *Confinia Psychiatrica* 23 (1980).

3. Jakob Wassermann, *The Maurizius Case*, trans. Caroline Newton (New York: Horace Liveright, 1929), 369.

4. Erik H. Erikson, *Young Man Luther: A Study in Psychoanalysis and History* (New York: W. W. Norton, 1958), 208.

5. Albert Speer, *Inside the Third Reich: Memoirs*, trans. Richard and Clara Winston (New York: Macmillan, 1970).

6. *The New York Times*, 2 September 1981.

7. Friedrich Percyval Reck-Malleczewen, *Diary of a Man in Despair*, trans. Paul Rubens (New York: Macmillan, 1970), 194.

8. Roger Manvell and Heinrich Fraenkel, *The Incomparable Crime: Mass Extermination in the 20th Century: The Legacy of Guilt* (London: Heinemann, 1967), 126.

9. Ibid., 127.

10. Ibid.

11. Ibid., 128.

12. Ibid., 122.

13. Ibid., 128.

14. Ibid., 49, 50.

15. Reported in a television interview with Adolf Eichmann's guards, Zweites Deutsches Fernsehen, 1 February 1980.

16. Hannah Arendt, *Eichmann in Jerusalem: A Report on the Banality of Evil* (New York: Penguin Books, 1977).

17. All biographical information about Klaus Barbie is from Magnus Linklater et al., *The Nazi Legacy: Klaus Barbie and the International Fascist Connection* (New York: Holt, Rinehart and Winston, 1985); and Francine du Plessix Gray, "The Progress of Klaus Barbie," *The New York Review of Books*, 27 June 1985.

18. Alexander and Margarete Mitscherlich, *The Inability to Mourn: Principles of Collective Behavior*, trans. Beverly R. Placzek (New York: Grove Press, 1975).

19. Jakob Wassermann, *The World's Illusion*, trans. Ludwig Lewisohn, 2 vols. (New York: Harcourt, Brace, 1935), 344–45.

Chapter III. The Covert Cult of Death

1. Wilhelm Kütemeyer, *Die Krankheit Europas: Beiträge zu einer Morphologie* (Berlin: Suhrkamp, 1951), 124–25.

2. Ibid., 126–27.

3. Ibid., 128.

4. Manvell and Fraenkel, *The Incomparable Crime*, 43.

5. Helmut Krausnick et al. *Anatomy of the SS State*, trans. Richard Barry, Marian Jackson, and Dorothy Long (London: Granada, 1982), 138.

6. Ernst von Schenk, *Europa vor der deutschen Frage: Briefe eines Schweizers nach Deutschland* (Berne: Francke, 1946), 142.

7. "Vietnam Horror Haunts Deserter," *The New York Post*, 23 December 1971.

8. Manvell and Fraenkel, *The Incomparable Crime*, 141.

9. Stanley Milgram, *Obedience to Authority: An Experimental View* (New York: Harper & Row, 1974). See also Gruen, *Betrayal of the Self*, 24–25.

10. Manvell and Fraenkel, *The Incomparable Crime*, 181.

11. Daniel Tranel and Antonio R. Damasio, "Knowledge without Awareness: An Autonomic Index of Facial Recognition by Prosopagnosics," *Science* 228 (21 June 1985): 1453–54.

12. Oliver Sacks, "The President's Speech," *The New York Review of Books*, 15 August 1985.

13. Ibid.

14. Ibid.

15. Ibid.

16. Ibid.

17. Mitscherlich and Mitscherlich, *The Inability to Mourn.*

18. von Schenck, *Europa vor der deutschen Frage,* 140.

19. Ibid., 140–41.

20. "Coed Kills Herself over Pet Dog Doomed by Father," *The New York Times,* 7 February 1968.

21. H. C. Kirsch, ed., *Der spanische Bürgerkrieg in Augenzeugenberichten* (Munich: Deutscher Taschenbuch Verlag, 1986), 144.

22. Kütemeyer, *Die Krankheit Europas,* 130.

23. Albert Speer, *Spandau: The Secret Diaries,* trans. Richard and Clara Winston (New York: Macmillan, 1976), 80.

24. Ernst Jünger, *Strahlungen III* (Munich: Deutscher Taschenbuch Verlag, 1966), 23. Saul Friedländer also emphasizes this point in *Reflections of Naziism: An Essay on Kitsch and Death,* trans. Thomas Weyr (New York: Harper & Row, 1984).

25. Luise Rinser, *Don Wolf umarmen* (Frankfurt: Fischer, 1981), 290.

26. Speer, *Inside the Third Reich,* 479–80.

27. M. Siirala, *From Transfer to Transference,* 115.

Chapter IV. Feelings That Are Not Feelings

1. All of the citations about the case of Gregg Sanders in the following pages are drawn from two contemporary newspaper articles: "Jersey Boy, 15, Kills Parents," *The New York Times,* 16 January 1975. "Boy Who Killed Parents and Himself Led Secret, Tormented Life," *The New York Times,* 3 February 1975.

2. Sigmund Freud, *An Outline of Psycho-Analysis,* vol. 23 of *The Standard Edition of the Complete Psychological Works of Sigmund Freud,* trans. and ed. James Strachey (London: The Hogarth Press and the Institute of Psychoanalysis, 1981), 148.

3. T. C. Schneirla, "Interrelationships of the 'Innate' and the 'Acquired' in Instinctive Behavior," in *L'Instinct dans le comportement des animaux et de l'homme,* ed. Pierre Paul Grassé (Paris: Masson, 1956). David S. Lehrman, "A Critique of Lorenz's 'Objectivistic' Theory of Animal Behavior," *Quarterly Review of Biology* 28, no. 4 (December 1953), 359.

200   *Notes*

4. *The New York Times*, 4, 14, 17 October 1971. Tom Wicker, "What Was the Hurry?" *The New York Times*, 19 January 1971. Malcolm Bell, *The Turkey Shoot* (New York: Grove Press, 1985). The description of events at Attica given in the text comes from these sources.

5. M. Schwander, "Mundartpoet wird als 'Drachentöter' bejubelt," *Tages-Anzeiger* (Switzerland), 10 December 1985.

6. Henry T. Nash, "The Bureaucratization of Homicide," *The Bulletin of the Atomic Scientists* 36, no. 4 (1980): 22–27.

7. Ibid.

8. Ibid.

9. George W. S. Trow, "Annals of Discourse: The Harvard Black Rock Forest," *The New Yorker*, 11 June 1984, 49–50.

10. Ibid.

11. Ibid.

12. Ibid.

13. Natalya Viktorovna Hesse, "The Sakharovs in Gorky," *The New York Review of Books*, 12 April 1984.

14. Countess Sybil Schönfeldt, "Ich war Arbeitsmaid," *Die Zeit*, 20 September 1985.

15. Ibid.

16. C. Turkington, "High Court Weighs Value of Research by Social Scientists," *The American Psychological Association Monitor*, 17 February 1986.

17. Ibid.

18. Seymour M. Hersh, *My Lai 4: A Report on the Massacre and Its Aftermath* (New York: Random House, 1970).

19. Robert Jay Lifton, "Reviews of the My Lai 4 and Son My Massacres," *The New York Times Book Review*, 14 June 1970.

20. William Wright, *The von Bülow Affair* (New York: Delacorte, 1983). Ann Jones, "Murder and Sympathy," *The Nation*, 17 September 1983.

21. Wright, *von Bülow Affair*. Jones, "Murder and Sympathy."

22. Willard Gaylin, *The Killing of Bonnie Garland: A Question of Justice* (New York: Simon & Schuster, 1982). Robert Coles, "Justice," *The New Yorker*, 26 July 1982, 92.

23. Coles, "Justice."

24. Ibid.

25. David S. Wyman, *The Abandonment of the Jews: America and the Holocaust 1941–1945* (New York: Pantheon Books, 1984).

26. "90-Kilo-Rabenmutter wurde freigesprochen," *Tages-Anzeiger* (Switzerland), 10 March 1983.

27. David Bakan, *Slaughter of the Innocents* (San Francisco: Jossey-Bass, 1971).

28. David G. Gil, *Physical Child Abuse in the United States* (Cambridge: Harvard Univ. Press, 1970).

29. "AI—Kinder als Opfer von Folter und Terror," *Basler Zeitung*, 15 October 1979.

30. Notes and Comments, *The New Yorker*, 29 July 1985.

31. "Gasversuche in Dachau," *Nebelspalter* (Rorschach, Switzerland), October 1981.

32. "Sanctuary," *The New Yorker*, 30 June 1986, 24.

33. Ibid.

34. Ibid.

35. "Auch bei drohender Folter kein Recht auf Asyl," *Tages-Anzeiger* (Switzerland), 24 September 1985.

36. "Duisberg—Milde Strafen fur fünf Fussballrowdies," *Tages-Anzeiger* (Zurich), 28 November 1985.

Chapter V. Conformity, Rebellion, and Violence

1. Georgii Valentinovich Plekhanov, *The Role of the Individual in History* (New York: International Publishers, 1940), 58.

2. Russell Jacoby, *Social Amnesia: A Critique of Conformist Psychology from Adler to Laing* (Boston: Beacon Press, 1975).

3. Barry Hindess and Paul Q. Hirst, *Pre-Capitalist Modes of Production* (London and Boston: Routledge and Paul, 1975), 310–12.

4. E. P. Thompson, *The Poverty of Theory and Other Essays* (New York and London: Monthly Review Press, 1978).

5. John K. Antill and John D. Cunningham, "Self-Esteem as a Function of Masculinity in Both Sexes," *Journal of Consulting and Clinical Psychology* 47, no. 4 (1979): 785.

6. David A. Ward and Gene G. Kassebaum, *Women's Prison: Sex and Social Structure* (Chicago: Aldene, 1965).

7. Ralph H. Gundlach, "Childhood Parental Relationships and the Establishment of Gender Roles of Homosexuals," *Journal of Consulting and Clinical Psychology* 33 (1969).

8. Ronald V. Sampson, *The Psychology of Power* (New York: Pantheon Books, 1966), 100.

9. Samuel Butler, *The Way of All Flesh* (London: Oxford Univ. Press, 1951), 106–7.

10. Ann Roskam, "Patterns of Autonomy in High Achieving Adolescent Girls Who Differ in Need for Approval" (Ph.D. diss., City Univ. of New York, 1972).

11. Helen Bluvol, "Differences in Patterns of Autonomy in Achieving and Underachieving Adolescent Boys" (Ph.D. diss., City Univ. of New York, 1972).

12. Roskam, "Patterns of Autonomy."

13. Bluvol, "Differences in Patterns of Autonomy."

14. "Letter from Argentina," *The New Yorker*, 21 July 1986.

15. V. S. Naipaul, "Among the Republicans," *The New York Review of Books*, 25 October 1984.

16. Ibid.

17. Ibid.

18. Ibid.

19. Ibid.

20. Ibid.

21. Giovanni di Lorenzo, *Stefan, 22, deutscher Rechtsterrorist: "Mein Traum ist der Traum von vielen"* (Reinbek: Rowohlt, 1984).

22. Letter to the Editor, *The Manchester Guardian Weekly* (London), 11 September 1971.

23. di Lorenzo, *Stefan*, 48.

24. Ibid., 8.

25. Ibid., 36.

26. Ibid., 151.

27. Ibid., 78.

28. Ibid., 117–18.

29. Ibid., 146.

30. Ibid., 147.

31. Ibid., 147–50.

32. Ibid., 151, 153–54.

33. Norman Cohn, *The Pursuit of the Millennium: Revolutionary Messianism in Medieval and Reformation Europe and Its Bearing on Modern Totalitarian Movements*, 2nd ed. (New York: Harper & Row, 1961).

34. Ibid.

35. John Bushnell, *Mutiny Amid Repression* (Bloomington: Indiana Univ. Press, 1985).

36. Ibid.

37. Cohn, *Pursuit of the Millennium*.

38. Cohn, *Pursuit of the Millennium*, 73.

39. Ibid., 71.

40. H. Miller, *Time of the Assassins*, 48.

41. Ibid., 49.

42. Ibid., 49–50.

43. Ibid., 51.

44. Vladimir I. Lenin, "Left-Wing Communism—An Infantile Disorder," in vol. 31 of *Collected Works* (London: Lawrence & Wishart, 1966), 104.

45. Michael Baumann, *Terror or Love? Bommi Baumann's Own Story of His Life as a West German Urban Guerrilla*, with statements by Heinrich Böll and Daniel Cohn-Bendit, trans. Helene Ellenbogen and Wayne Parker (New York: Grove Press, 1977), 115.

46. H. Miller, *Time of the Assassins*, 51.

47. Paolo Freire, *Pedagogy of the Oppressed*, trans. Myra Bergman Ramos (New York: Continuum Press, 1986), 31.

48. Peter Schneider, "Gespräche eines Schiffbrüchigen mit einem Bewohner des Festlandes," *Die Zeit*, 5 April 1985.

49. Ibid.

50. Heinrich Böll, "Stimme aus dem Untergrund: Über Bommi Baumann, 'Wie alles anfing,'" *Konkret*, 29 January 1976. This statement also appears in Heinrich Böll, "Es kann einem bange werden," in *Schriften und Reden 1976–1977* (Munich: Deutscher Taschenbuch Verlag, 1985), 23–26.

51. Antonio Negri, *Sabotage* (Munich: Trikont, 1979), 64.

52. R. Luyken, "Die Schlacht der Fans," *Die Zeit*, 29 March 1985.

53. Ibid.

54. Wilfried Kratz, "Die 'Verlorenen' von Kirkby," *Die Zeit*, 26 April 1985.

55. Ibid.

56. Michael Harrington, "The New Lost Generation: Jobless Youth," *The New York Times Magazine*, 24 May 1964.

57. Kratz, "Die 'Verlorenen' von Kirkby."

58. Henry S. F. Cooper, Jr., "Letter from the Space Center," *The New Yorker*, 10 November 1986. "Commission Finds Flaws in NASA Decision-Making," *Science* 231 (14 March 1986). "New

Shuttle Director Promises Emphasis on Safety," *Science* 232 (11 April 1986). "Inquiry Faults Shuttle Management," *Science* 232 (20 July 1986).

59. Bertolt Brecht, *The Threepenny Opera*. Passage translated by Hildegarde and Hunter Hannum.

60. Charles E. Silberman, *Criminal Violence, Criminal Justice* (New York: Random House, 1978), 87–165.

61. G. Hielscher, "Gewalt an Japans Schulen nimmt zu," *Tages-Anzeiger* (Switzerland), 17 December 1985.

62. E. Heidenreich, "Über Aggression," *Brigitte*, 30 April 1986.

63. Muriel Hirsch, "To Sir, with Hate," *New Statesman* (London), 20 October 1972.

64. Ibid.

65. Ibid.

66. Jacobo Timerman, *Prisoner Without a Name, Cell Without a Number*, trans. Toby Talbot (New York: Vintage, 1982), 50.

67. Ibid., 95.

68. Wole Soyinka, *The Man Died* (New York: Harper & Row, 1972), 32, 80.

69. Ibid., 99.

70. M. Gray, *Der Schrei nach Leben: Die Geschichte eines Mannes, der die Unmenschlichkeit besiegte, weil er an die Menschen glaubte* (Berne: Scherz, 1980), 109.

Chapter VI. Power Politics as an Expression of Inner Emptiness

1. Richard M. Nixon, *No More Vietnams* (New York: Arbor House, 1985), 156, 157.

2. Stanley Karnow, *Vietnam: A History* (New York: Viking Press, 1983), 652.

3. Nixon, *No More Vietnams*, 145, 147.

4. Henry Kissinger, *White House Years* (Boston: Little, Brown, 1979), 1408, 1470.

5. Ronald Steel, "The Ancient Mariner," *The New York Review of Books*, 30 May 1985.

6. Nixon, *No More Vietnams*, 152.

7. Harry G. Summers, *On Strategy: A Critical Analysis of the Vietnam War* (Novato, Calif.: Presidio Press, 1982), 1.

8. Barbara W. Tuchman, *The March of Folly: From Troy to Vietnam* (New York: Alfred A. Knopf, 1984), 32.

9. Horst Eberhard Richter, *Die Chance des Gewissens: Erinnerungen und Assoziationen* (Hamburg: Hoffmann und Campe, 1986), 13.

10. Tuchman, *March of Folly*, 217.

11. Ibid., 192.

12. Ibid., 288.

13. Ibid.

14. Ibid., 293.

15. Ibid., 302.

16. Ibid., 303.

17. Carl Sandburg, *Abraham Lincoln: The War Years*, 2 vols. (New York: Dell, 1968).

18. Ibid., 658.

19. Ibid., 195.

20. Ibid., 381.

21. Umberto Eco, *The Name of the Rose*, trans. William Weaver (New York: Harcourt Brace Jovanovich, 1983), 370.

22. Michael Paul Rogin, *Ronald Reagan, the Movie and Other Episodes in Political Demonology* (Berkeley: Univ. of California Press, 1987).

23. Ibid.

24. Ibid.

25. Ronald Reagan with Richard G. Hubler, *Where's the Rest of Me?* (New York: Duell, Sloan and Pearce, 1965), 6–7.

26. Ibid.

27. Volker Elis Pilgrim, *Muttersöhne* (Düsseldorf: Claassen, 1986), 21.

28. Ibid., 39.

29. Ibid.

30. Rudolph Binion, *Hitler Among the Germans* (New York: Elsevier, 1976), 18. Pilgrim, *Muttersöhne*, 28.

31. Pilgrim, *Muttersöhne*, 34.

32. Binion, *Hitler Among the Germans*, 19.

33. Ibid., 18.

34. Rogin, *Ronald Reagan*, 34.

35. George W. Ball, "The War for Star Wars," *The New York Review of Books*, 11 April 1985.

36. See Alexander Haig, *Caveat: Realism, Reagan, and Foreign Policy* (New York: Macmillan, 1984).

37. Richard M. Nixon, *RN: The Memoirs of Richard Nixon* (New York: Grosset and Dunlap, 1978), 6, 8.

38. Ibid., 3–4.

39. H. U. Thamer, *Verführung und Gewalt: Deutschland 1933–1945* (Berlin: Siedler, 1986), 72.

40. Ibid.

41. Count Harry Kessler, *Walter Rathenau: His Life and Work*, trans. W. D. Robson-Scott and Lawrence Hyde (New York: Howard Fertig, 1969), 17.

42. Thamer, *Verführung und Gewalt*, 75.

43. Robert G. Kaiser, "Your Host of Hosts," *The New York Review of Books*, 28 June 1984.

44. Murray Kempton, "The Great Lobbyist," *The New York Review of Books*, 17 February 1983.

Chapter VII. The Psychopath and Peer Gynt

1. Hervey Cleckley, *The Mask of Insanity* (St. Louis: Mosby, 1964), 404–6.

2. Ibid., 406–7.

3. Steel, "Ancient Mariner."

4. Henrik Ibsen, *Peer Gynt*, trans. Michael Meyer (Garden City: Anchor Books, 1963). All passages are quoted from this edition.

5. Cleckley, *Mask of Insanity*, 187–89.

6. Ibid., 189–90.

7. V. Arpe, ed., *Henrik Ibsen: Part I*, Dichter über ihre Dichtungen, 10/1 (Munich: Heimeran, 1972), 164–65.

8. The Talk of the Town, *The New Yorker*, 25 March 1985, 35.

9. Arno Gruen, "The Discontinuity in the Ontogeny of Self: Possibilities for Integration or Destructiveness," *Psychoanalytic Review* 61 (1974/75).

10. Cited in Laing, *Divided Self*, 123–24.

11. Ibid., 124–25.

12. Ellen Glasgow, *The Woman Within* (New York: Harcourt, Brace, 1954), 3–4.

13. George Victor, *The Riddle of Autism: A Psychological*

Analysis (Lexington, Massachusetts: Lexington Books, 1983). Gruen and Prekop, "Das Festhalten und die Problematik der Bindung im Autismus."

14. Glasgow, *Woman Within*, 3–4.

15. Sampson, *Psychology of Power*, 30.

16. Paul Schilder, *The Image and Appearance of the Human Body: Studies in the constructive energies of the psyche* (New York: International Universities Press, 1950), 267.

17. Doris Beckord, "Körperbild und Körperleben in der Schwangerschaft" (Paper presented at the Seventh Conference of the Internationale Studiengemeinschaft für Pränatale Psychologie, Düsseldorf, 1983). Cf. also Doris Beckord, "Theorie und Praxis der Körperbildforschung mit einer empirischen Untersuchung zum Körperleben in der Schwangerschaft" (Diss., Univ. of Salzburg, 1983).

18. Lee N. Robins et al., "Lifetime Prevalence of Specific Psychiatric Disorders in Three Sites," *Archives of General Psychiatry* 41 (October 1984), 949.

Chapter VIII. Insanity as Way of Life, Insanity as Protest

1. Roland Kirbach, "Die furchtbaren Bürokraten," *Die Zeit*, 24 August 1984.

2. *The New York Times*, June 11, 1985.

3. The Talk of the Town, *The New Yorker*, 11 November 1985.

4. Ibid.

5. Milan Kundera, *The Book of Laughter and Forgetting*, trans. Michael Heim (New York: Alfred A. Knopf, 1980), 3.

6. Joseph Lelyveld, "The Enduring Legacy," *The New York Times Magazine*, 31 March 1985, 35.

7. Martti Siirala, "Psychotherapy of Schizophrenia as a Basic Human Experience, as a Ferment for a Metamorphosis in the Conception of Knowledge and the Image of Man," in *Psychotherapy of Schizophrenia*, ed. D. Rubinstein and Y. O. Alanen (Amsterdam: Excerpta Medica, 1972), 141.

8. M. Siirala, *From Transfer to Transference*, 35.

9. Barbara O'Brien, *Operators and Things: The Inner Life of a Schizophrenic* (Cambridge, Massachusetts: Arlington Books, 1958), 148.

10. Ibid., 149.
11. Ibid., 150.
12. Ibid., 151.
13. Ibid., 31.
14. Ibid., 152.
15. Ibid., 148.
16. Ibid., 154.

Bibliography

Antill, John K., and John D. Cunningham. "Self-Esteem as a Function of Masculinity in Both Sexes." *Journal of Consulting and Clinical Psychology* 47, no. 4 (1979).

Arendt, Hannah. *Eichmann in Jerusalem: A Report on the Banality of Evil.* New York: Penguin Books, 1977.

Aronson, Eric, and Shelley Rosenbloom. "Space Perception in Early Infancy: Perception within a Common Auditory-Visual Space." *Science* 172 (11 June 1971).

Arpe, V., ed. *Henrik Ibsen: Part I.* Dichter über ihre Dichtungen, 10/1. Munich: Heimeran, 1972.

Ascherson, Neal. "The 'Bildung' of Barbie." *The New York Review of Books*, 24 November 1983.

Bakan, David. *Slaughter of the Innocents.* San Francisco: Jossey-Bass, 1971.

Ball, George W. "The War for Star Wars." *The New York Review of Books*, 11 April 1985.

Baumann, Michael. *Terror or Love? Bommi Baumann's Own Story of His Life as a West German Urban Guerrilla.* With statements by Heinrich Böll and Daniel Cohn-Bendit. Translated by Helene Ellenbogen and Wayne Parker. New York: Grove Press, 1977.

Beckord, Doris. "Körperbild und Körperleben in der Schwangerschaft." Paper presented to the Seventh conference of the Internationale Studiengemeinschaft für Pränatale Psychologie, Düsseldorf, 1983.

———. "Theorie und Praxis der Körperbildforschung mit einer empirischen Untersuchung zum Körperleben in der Schwangerschaft." Diss., University of Salzburg, 1983.

Bell, Malcolm. *The Turkey Shoot.* New York: Grove Press, 1985.

Benedetti, Gaetano. *The Psychotherapy of Schizophrenia.* New York: New York Univ. Press, 1987.

Bertini, M. et al. "Intrauterine Mechanisms of Synchronization: In Search of the First Dialogue." *Totus Homo* 8 (1978).

Bettelheim, Bruno. *The Empty Fortress: Infantile Autism and the Birth of the Self.* New York: Free Press, 1967.

Binion, Rudolph. *Hitler Among the Germans.* New York: Elsevier, 1976.

Bluvol, Helen. "Differences in Patterns of Autonomy in Achieving and Underachieving Adolescent Boys." Ph.D. diss., City University of New York, 1972.

Böll, Heinrich. "Es kann einem bange werden." In *Schriften und Reden 1976–1977.* Munich: Deutscher Taschenbuch Verlag, 1985.

————. "Stimme aus dem Untergrund: Über Bommi Baumann, 'Wie alles anfing.'" *Konkret,* 29 January 1976.

Brecht, Bertolt. *The Threepenny Opera.* Passage translated by Hildegarde and Hunter Hannum.

Bushnell, John. *Mutiny Amid Repression.* Bloomington: Indiana Univ. Press, 1985.

Butler, Samuel. *The Way of All Flesh.* London: Oxford Univ. Press, 1951.

Bychowski, Gustav. "Struggle Against the Introjects." *International Journal of Psycho-Analysis* 39 (1958).

Cameron, James R. "Parental Treatment, Children's Temperament, and the Risk of Childhood Behavior Problems." *American Journal of Orthopsychiatry* 47 (1977).

Cleckley, Hervey. *The Mask of Insanity.* St. Louis: Mosby, 1964.

Cohn, Norman. *The Pursuit of the Millennium: Revolutionary Messianism in Medieval and Reformation Europe and Its Bearing on Modern Totalitarian Movements.* New York: Harper & Row, 1961.

Coles, Robert. "Justice." *The New Yorker,* 26 July 1982.

Cooper, Henry S. F., Jr. "Letter from the Space Center." *The New Yorker,* 10 November 1986.

Eco, Umberto. *The Name of the Rose.* Translated by William Weaver. New York: Harcourt Brace Jovanovich, 1983.

Erikson, Erik H. *Young Man Luther: A Study in Psychoanalysis and History.* New York: W. W. Norton, 1958.

Freire, Paulo. *Pedagogy of the Oppressed.* Translated by Myra Bergman Ramos. New York: Continuum Press, 1986.

Freud, Sigmund. *Beyond the Pleasure Principle.* Vol. 18 of *Standard Edition of the Complete Psychological Works of Sigmund Freud,* translated and edited by James Strachey. London: The Hogarth Press and the Institute of Psychoanalysis, 1961.

_____. *Civilization and Its Discontents.* Vol. 21 of *Standard Edition,* 1981.

_____. *New Introductory Lectures on Psycho-Analysis.* Vol. 22 of *Standard Edition,* 1971.

_____. *An Outline of Psycho-Analysis.* Vol. 23 of *Standard Edition,* 1981.

_____. *Three Essays on the Theory of Sexuality.* Vol. 7 of *Standard Edition,* 1953.

Friedländer, Saul. *Reflections of Naziism: An Essay on Kitsch and Death.* Translated by Thomas Weyr. New York: Harper & Row, 1984.

Fromm, Erich. *The Anatomy of Human Destructiveness.* New York: Holt, Rinehart and Winston, 1973.

Gaylin, Willard. *The Killing of Bonnie Garland: A Question of Justice.* New York: Simon & Schuster, 1982.

Gelb, Barbara, and Arthur. *O'Neill.* New York: Harper & Row, 1973.

Gil, David G. *Physical Child Abuse in the United States.* Cambridge: Harvard Univ. Press, 1970.

Glasgow, Ellen. *The Woman Within.* New York: Harcourt, Brace, 1954.

Gray, Francine du Plessix. "The Progress of Klaus Barbie." *The New York Review of Books,* 27 June 1985.

Gray, M. *Der Schrei nach Leben: Die Geschichte eines Mannes, der die Unmenschlichkeit besiegte, weil er an die Menschen glaubte.* Berne: Scherz, 1980.

Gruen, Arno. "Autonomy and Compliance: The Fundamental Antithesis." *Journal of Humanistic Psychology* 16, no. 3 (1976).

_____. *The Betrayal of the Self: The Fear of Autonomy in Men and Women.* With preface by Gaetano Benedetti and foreword by Ashley Montagu. Translated by Hildegarde and Hunter Hannum. New York: Grove Press, 1986.

————. "The Discontinuity in the Ontogeny of Self: Possibilities for Integration or Destructiveness." *Psychoanalytic Review* 61 (1974/75).

————. *Der frühe Abschied: Eine Deutung des Plötzlichen Kindstodes.* With foreword by Ashley Montagu. Munich: Kösel, 1988.

————. "Maternal Rejection and Children's Intensity: Implications for Sex Differences in Affective Development." *Confinia Psychiatrica* 23 (1980).

Gruen, Arno, and Jirina Prekop. "Das Festhalten und die Problematik der Bindung im Autismus: Theoretische Betrachtungen." *Praxis der Kinderpsychologie und Kinderpsychiatrie* 7 (1986).

Gundlach, Ralph H. "Childhood Parental Relationships and the Establishment of Gender Roles of Homosexuals." *Journal of Consulting and Clinical Psychology* 33 (1969).

Haig, Alexander. *Caveat: Realism, Reagan, and Foreign Policy.* New York: Macmillan, 1984.

Harrington, Michael. "The New Lost Generation: Jobless Youth." *The New York Times Magazine*, 24 May 1964.

Heidenreich, E. "Über Aggression." *Brigitte*, 30 April 1986.

Hersh, Seymour M. *My Lai 4: A Report on the Massacre and Its Aftermath.* New York: Random House, 1970.

Hesse, Natalya Viktorovna. "The Sakharovs in Gorky." *The New York Review of Books*, 12 April 1984.

Hindess, Barry, and Paul Q. Hirst. *Pre-Capitalist Modes of Production.* London and Boston: Routledge and Paul, 1975.

Hirsch, Muriel. "To Sir, With Hate." *New Statesman* (London), 20 October 1972.

Hoover, Carol F. "Prolonged Schizophrenia and the Will." *Journal of Humanistic Psychology* 11 (1971).

Ibsen, Henrik. *Peer Gynt.* Translated by Michael Meyer. Garden City: Anchor Books, 1963.

Jacoby, Russell. *Social Amnesia: A Critique of Conformist Psychology from Adler to Laing.* Boston: Beacon Press, 1975.

Jones, Ann. "Murder and Sympathy." *The Nation*, 17 September 1983.

Jünger, Ernst. *Strahlungen III*. Munich: Deutscher Taschenbuch Verlag, 1966.

Kaiser, Robert G. "Your Host of Hosts." *The New York Review of Books*, 28 June 1984.

Karnow, Stanley. *Vietnam: A History*. New York: Viking Press, 1983.

Kempton, Murray. "The Great Lobbyist." *The New York Review of Books*, 17 February 1983.

Kessler, Count Harry. *Walter Rathenau: His Life and Work*. Translated by W. D. Robson-Scott and Lawrence Hyde. New York: Howard Fertig, 1969.

Kirsch, H. C., ed. *Der spanische Bürgerkrieg in Augenzeugen-berichten*. Munich: Deutscher Taschenbuch Verlag, 1986.

Kissinger, Henry. *White House Years*. Boston: Little, Brown, 1979.

Krausnick, Helmut, Hans Buchheim, Martin Broszat, and Hans-Adolf Jacobsen. *Anatomy of the SS State*. Translated by Richard Barry, Marian Jackson, and Dorothy Long. London: Granada, 1982.

Kundera, Milan. *The Book of Laughter and Forgetting*. Translated by Michael Heim. New York: Alfred A. Knopf, 1980.

Kütemeyer, Wilhelm. *Die Krankheit Europas: Beiträge zu einer Morphologie*. Berlin: Suhrkamp, 1951.

Laing, Ronald David. *The Divided Self: A Study of Sanity and Madness*. Chicago: Quadrangle Books, 1960.

Lehrman, David S. "A Critique of Lorenz's 'Objectivistic' Theory of Animal Behavior." *Quarterly Review of Biology* 28, no. 4 (December 1953).

Lelyveld, Joseph. "The Enduring Legacy." *The New York Times Magazine*, 31 March 1985.

Lenin, Vladimir I. "Left-Wing Communism—An Infantile Disorder." In Vol. 31 of *Collected Works*. London: Lawrence & Wishart, 1966.

Lifton, Robert Jay. "Reviews of the My Lai 4 and Son My Massacres." *The New York Times Book Review*, 14 June 1970.

Linklater, Magnus et al. *The Nazi Legacy: Klaus Barbie and the International Fascist Connection*. New York: Holt, Rinehart and Winston, 1985.

Lorenzo, Giovanni di. *Stefan, 22, deutscher Rechtsterrorist: "Mein Traum ist der Traum von vielen."* Reinbek: Rowohlt, 1984.

Manvell, Roger, and Heinrich Fraenkel. *The Incomparable Crime: Mass Extermination in the Twentieth Century: The Legacy of Guilt.* London: Heinemann, 1967.

Milgram, Stanley. *Obedience to Authority: An Experimental View.* New York: Harper & Row, 1974.

Miller, Alice. *The Drama of the Gifted Child: How Narcissistic Parents Form and Deform the Emotional Lives of Their Talented Children.* Originally published as *Prisoners of Childhood.* Translated by Ruth Ward. New York: Basic Books, 1981.

_____. *For Your Own Good: Hidden Cruelty in Child-Rearing and the Roots of Violence.* Translated by Hildegarde and Hunter Hannum. New York: Farrar, Straus and Giroux, 1983.

Miller, Henry. *The Time of the Assassins: A Study of Rimbaud.* New York: New Directions, 1962.

Mitscherlich, Alexander, and Margarete. *The Inability to Mourn.* Translated by Beverly R. Placzek. New York: Grove Press, 1975.

Naipaul, V. S. "Among the Republicans." *The New York Review of Books,* 25 October 1984.

Nash, Henry T. "The Bureaucratization of Homicide." *The Bulletin of Atomic Scientists* 36, no. 4 (1980).

Negri, Antonio. *Sabotage.* Munich: Trikont, 1979.

Nixon, Richard M. *No More Vietnams.* New York: Arbor House, 1985.

_____. *RN: The Memoirs of Richard Nixon.* New York: Grosset and Dunlap, 1978.

O'Brien, Barbara. *Operators and Things: The Inner Life of a Schizophrenic.* Cambridge, Massachusetts: Arlington Books, 1958.

Pilgrim, Volker Elis. *Muttersöhne.* Düsseldorf: Claassen, 1986.

Plekhanov, Georgii Valentinovich. *The Role of the Individual in History.* New York: International Publishers, 1940.

Polyani, Michael. *Personal Knowledge: Towards a Post-Critical Philosophy.* Chicago: Univ. of Chicago Press, 1960.

Prekop, Jirina. "Frühkindlicher Autismus." *Offenes Gesundheitswesen* 44 (1982).

Reagan, Ronald, with Richard G. Hubler. *Where's the Rest of Me?* New York: Duell, Sloan and Pearce, 1965.

Reck-Malleczewen, Friedrich Percyval. *Diary of a Man in De-*

spair. Translated by Paul Rubens. New York: Macmillan, 1970.

Ribble, Margaretha A. *The Rights of Infants: Early Psychological Needs and Their Satisfaction.* New York: Columbia Univ. Press, 1943.

Richter, Horst Eberhard. *Die Chance des Gewissens: Erinnerungen und Assoziationen.* Hamburg: Hoffmann und Campe, 1986.

Rinser, Luise. *Den Wolf umarmen.* Frankfurt: Fischer, 1981.

Robins, Lee N. "Lifetime Prevalence of Specific Psychiatric Disorders in Three Sites." *Archives of General Psychiatry* 41 (October 1984).

Rogin, Michael Paul. *Ronald Reagan, the Movie and Other Episodes in Political Demonology.* Berkeley: Univ. of California Press, 1987.

Roskam, Ann. "Patterns of Autonomy in High Achieving Adolescent Girls Who Differ in Need for Approval." Ph.D. diss., City University of New York, 1972.

Sacks, Oliver. "The President's Speech." *The New York Review of Books,* 15 August 1985.

Sampson, Ronald V. *The Psychology of Power.* New York: Pantheon Books, 1966.

Sandburg, Carl. *Abraham Lincoln: The War Years.* 2 vols. New York: Dell, 1968.

Schenk, Ernst von. *Europa vor der deutschen Frage: Briefe eines Schweizers nach Deutschland.* Berne: Francke, 1946.

Schilder, Paul. *The Image and Appearance of the Human Body: Studies in the constructive energies of the psyche.* New York: International Universities Press, 1950.

Schneirla, T. C. "An Evolutionary and Developmental Theory of Biphasic Processes Underlying Approach and Withdrawal." In *Nebraska Symposium on Motivation,* edited by Marshall R. Jones. Lincoln, Neb.: Univ. of Nebraska Press, 1959.

————. "Interrelationships of the 'Innate' and the 'Acquired' in Instinctive Behavior." In *L'Instinct dans le comportement des animaux et de l'homme,* edited by Pierre Paul Grassé. Paris: Masson, 1956.

Shaheen, E. "Failure to Thrive: A Retrospective Profile." *Clinical Pediatry* 7 (1968).

Siirala, Aarne. *Divine Humanness*. Philadelphia: Fortress Press, 1970.

_____. *The Voice of Illness*. Philadelphia: Fortress Press, 1964.

Siirala, Martti. "Psychotherapy of Schizophrenia as a Basic Human Experience, as a Ferment for a Metamorphosis in the Conception of Knowledge and the Image of Man." In *Psychotherapy of Schizophrenia*, edited by D. Rubinstein and Y. O. Alanen. Amsterdam: Excerpta Medica, 1972.

_____. *From Transfer to Transference*. Helsinki: Therapeia Foundation, 1983.

_____. "Was macht Gewalt bösartig?" Paper delivered to the Deutsche Psychoanalytische Gesellschaft, Berlin, 13 November 1985.

Silberman, Charles E. *Criminal Violence, Criminal Justice*. New York: Random House, 1978.

Soyinka, Wole. *The Man Died*. New York: Harper & Row, 1972.

Speer, Albert. *Inside the Third Reich: Memoirs*. Translated by Richard and Clara Winston. New York: Macmillan, 1970.

_____. *Spandau: The Secret Diaries*. Translated by Richard and Clara Winston. New York: Macmillan, 1976.

Steel, Ronald. "The Ancient Mariner." *The New York Review of Books*, 30 May 1985.

Sullivan, Harry Stack. *The Interpersonal Theory of Psychiatry*. New York: W. W. Norton, 1953.

Summers, Harry G. *On Strategy: A Critical Analysis of the Vietnam War*. Novato, Calif.: Presidio Press, 1982.

Thamer, H. U. *Verführung und Gewalt: Deutschland 1933–1945*. Berlin: Siedler, 1986.

Thompson, E. P. *The Poverty of Theory and Other Essays*. New York and London: Monthly Review Press, 1978.

Timerman, Jacobo. *Prisoner Without a Name, Cell Without a Number*. Translated by Toby Talbot. New York: Vintage, 1982.

Tranel, Daniel, and Antonio R. Damasio. "Knowledge without Awareness: An Autonomic Index of Facial Recognition by Prosopagnosics." *Science* 228 (21 June 1985).

Trow, George W. S. "Annals of Discourse: The Harvard Black Rock Forest." *The New Yorker*, 11 June 1984.

Tuchman, Barbara W. *The March of Folly: From Troy to Vietnam.* New York: Alfred A. Knopf, 1984.

Turkington, C. "High Court Weighs Value of Research by Social Scientists." *American Psychological Association Monitor,* 17 February 1986.

Victor, George. *The Riddle of Autism: A Psychological Analysis.* Lexington, Massachusetts: Lexington Books, 1983.

Ward, David A., and Gene G. Kassebaum. *Women's Prison: Sex and Social Structure.* Chicago: Aldene, 1965.

Wassermann, Jakob. *The Maurizius Case.* Translated by Caroline Newton. New York: Horace Liveright, 1929.

_____. *The World's Illusion.* 2 vols. Translated by Ludwig Lewisohn. New York: Harcourt, Brace, 1935.

Wright, William. *The von Bülow Affair.* New York: Delacorte, 1983.

Wyman, David S. *The Abandonment of the Jews: America and the Holocaust 1941–1945.* New York: Pantheon Books, 1984.

Index